the PERSONAL TRAINER'S HANDBOOK

Teri S. O'Brien, MS, JD

Human Kinetics

Library of Congress Cataloging-in-Publication Data

O'Brien, Teri, 1955-
    The personal trainer's handbook / Teri O'Brien
        p.   cm.
    Includes bibliographical references (p.) and index.
    ISBN 0-88011-593-9
    1. Personal trainers--Handbooks, manuals, etc.   2. Personal
trainers--Vocational guidance--Handbooks, manuals, etc.   I. Title.
    GV428.7.037   1997
    613.7'1--dc20   96-41431
                                                                                              CIP

ISBN: 0-88011-593-9

Acquisitions Editor: Rick Frey, PhD; **Developmental Editor:** Nanette Smith; **Managing Editor:** Henry Woolsey; **Editorial Assistant:** Coree Schutter; **Copyeditor:** Jackie Blakley; **Proofreader:** Erin Cler; **Indexer:** Joan Griffitts; **Grapic Designer:** Stuart Cartwright; **Grapic Artist:** Tara Welsch; **Photo Editor:** Boyd LaFoon; **Cover Designer:** Stuart Cartwright; **Photographer (cover):** John Kelly; **Illustrator:** Marge Pavich; **Printer:** Versa Press

Printed in the United States of America   10   9   8   7   6   5   4   3

Human Kinetics
Web site: http://www.humankinetics.com/

United States: Human Kinetics, P.O. Box 5076, Champaign, IL 61825-5076
1-800-747-4457
e-mail: humank@hkusa.com

Canada: Human Kinetics, 475 Devonshire Road, Unit 100, Windsor, ON N8Y 2L5
1-800-465-7301 (in Canada only)
e-mail: humank@hkcanada.com

Europe: Human Kinetics, P.O. Box IW14, Leeds LS16 6TR, United Kingdom
(44) 1132 781708
e-mail: humank@hkeurope.com

Australia: Human Kinetics, 57A Price Avenue, Lower Mitcham, South Australia 5062
(088) 277 1555
e-mail: humank@hkaustralia.com

New Zealand: Human Kinetics, P.O. Box 105-231, Auckland 1
(09) 523 3462
e-mail: humank@hknewz.com

To the many conscientious, responsible health professionals who know that being a personal trainer means more than perkily chirping, "I'm Mindy! Lift your leg."

CONTENTS

Preface, or Why I Wrote This Book

After I began my personal training business, I began to get phone calls from my graduate school colleagues asking me questions—lots of questions. "How do I know whether to incorporate?" "Do I need liability insurance?" Even, "What *is* liability insurance?" Actually, they were all asking the same thing in a roundabout kind of way: "How did you get started, anyway?" After answering these questions over and over, I realized that I could write all of the answers down in one place and finally stop repeating myself. What a concept! The result of this thought is the book you're holding right now.

This book has a unique and wonderful feature—the Resistance Workout Guide. See, I've learned a lot of little tips that make many common resistance training exercises much more effective—pearls, I like to call them. For example, would you think to place a bench at the foot of the incline bench when instructing a client doing incline bench presses? I didn't at first. It's a little thing, but it can make a big difference in your client's comfort and back stability, not to mention boosting your reputation as someone who knows those extra little details that make you one of the best trainers around. It might take months or years to figure this out on your own, and it's not the kind of thing you'll see explained anywhere. That is, until now. The Resistance Workout Guide will give you lots of handy bits of information like that, as well as other pearls that will prove priceless in your work with clients.

The Resistance Workout Guide is based on the fundamental premise that the body is a system of pulleys and levers. Every movement involves at least one axis of rotation around which a lever or levers pivot after a force has been exerted by a muscle or muscles. If both you and your client understand this general concept and the specific axis (joint), lever (bone), and prime mover (muscle) for

each exercise, you'll dramatically increase the effectiveness of every exercise, every repetition, and every workout.

Not only does the Resistance Workout Guide provide vital biomechanical information, it applies that information to your training practice. What is the objective of this exercise? What are the practical implications for your client's form? What mistakes should she avoid? What form points should you check? The Resistance Workout Guide also notes exercises that are safe for some clients and contraindicated for others. All of this information is contained in a concise format on a single page for each exercise. Exercises are broken down into their basic parts, making them understandable. With the Resistance Workout Guide, good form is simple to teach and understand.

By now you're thinking that this book is the greatest thing since sliced bread and the last fitness book you'll ever need. To that I say you're correct on the first point but, as to that second one, hold your horses! *The Personal Trainer's Handbook* is a manual that will give you the basics you need to be a professional personal trainer. It isn't, and doesn't pretend to be, the last or only book a personal trainer needs. I strongly encourage you to consult the Suggested Reading section (p.173). You should also regularly review new books. Continuing education is one of the hallmarks of a true professional.

What this book is

- A practical reference for personal trainers and would-be personal trainers

- Chock-full of pearls, little hints about personal training practice

- An introduction to business and tax planning for

personal trainers designed to alert you to potential pitfalls and suggest ways to manage these important details

- A general discussion of legal issues facing personal trainers and methods of protecting yourself from potential problems

- A guide to designing safe, effective programs for your clients

- A comprehensive reference to the most frequently used resistance exercises, including all the information you need to properly instruct your client and avoid injuries

- A primer on sustaining client motivation

- A source of many helpful forms for you to use in working with your clients

What this book is not

- A comprehensive reference work covering every aspect of exercise, fitness, or strength training programs

- A summary of certification standards

- A complete tax and legal reference book

- A detailed manual of fitness assessment and testing procedures

- A physiology, biomechanics, or kinesiology textbook

What This Book Is Really About: The Personal Trainer's Mission

Being a personal trainer requires tactile skill, intelligence, academic training, practical experience, sound judgment, and outstanding communication skills. In addition, it requires commitment and understanding of the importance of your job. It's one thing to simply do an exercise for a certain number of repetitions; it's quite another to do the exercise in such a way that the targeted muscle or muscle groups are worked while vulnerable areas are protected from unnecessary stress. It's one thing to assemble and assign a list of twelve exercises to your clients; it's another to take the time to evaluate and serve each client as an individual, taking into account his needs, goals, and limitations.

Just as you can help your clients achieve optimal health and fitness, if you don't exercise care, you can diminish your clients' enthusiasm about exercise and cause them problems, even serious injuries. This manual will help you be the best personal trainer possible by teaching you proper program design, good client relations, and wise business practices. You will supply the intangibles: the care, concern, and personality that make your clients' workouts not only safe and effective, but fun!

My overall objective is to teach you how to be a true fitness professional, a recognized purveyor of scientifically based, effective programs with a loyal, extremely satisfied clientele. When people start thinking about hiring a personal trainer, as more and more of them are, and wonder, "Who can I call who really knows what she's talking about?" I want them to immediately think of you.

That's the story of *The Personal Trainer's Handbook*. So, if you want to consistently achieve the standard of excellence that will make you the best, most professional personal trainer you can be, read on.

ACKNOWLEDGMENTS

I would like to thank some of the individuals who helped produce this book you now hold in your hands.

Richard Frey, acquisitions editor at Human Kinetics, helped me write a good preface and convinced his colleagues to publish this book. To be published by a firm whose name means quality is a dream come true, and Rick made it happen.

Nanette Smith, developmental editor at Human Kinetics and a conscientious, on-top-of-everything person, took a raw manuscript and, with the help of a great copyeditor and the other talented folks at HK, turned it into a real book.

Dr. Wayne Westcott, one of the country's most renowned authorities on strength training, took the time to read the manuscript of an enthusiastic but unknown author and the effort to write a letter endorsing its publication. He exemplifies the observation that the bigger they are, the more they help others.

Dr. Thomas Sattler, my academic mentor and a bright, funny, energetic dynamo, has been an inspiration to his students and a joy to his friends.

Ellen Mandarino, a talented and creative graphic designer, never gave up her faith that this project would be completed (no matter how many times I changed things around). Her faith and encouragement sustained me on many a day.

Marge Pavich, who created the original drawings in the Resistance Workout Guide, maintained her sunny disposition in the face of the prodigious numbers of photographs I gave her as models for drawings ("Teri, I can't put your head on this guy's body!").

Steve Dahl, my friend and client, who told me to relax and let it happen, which, although it was not what I wanted to hear, it was exactly what I needed to hear.

Judy Tullis, of clear mind and thick skin and proprietor of the world's greatest secretarial service, somehow managed to keep me organized and otherwise saved my bacon on a regular basis. Someone was looking out for me on the day she became my friend.

Jay Nickleski, Mary Beckley, and Jo Cozzi helped with the pictures for the Resistance Workout Guide.

Barb Nevoral, Maryse Jerich, Kapila Anand, and Pramod Anand gave valued encouragement along the way.

Ron Lilek, my husband, my partner, and my friend—words are not enough.

Core Beliefs Behind Excellence in Personal Training

This book began with a vision and a set of core beliefs that preceded my entry into the personal training business, which I hope will become clear to you as you read on.

I used to close my eyes and visualize working as a knowledgeable, well-educated health professional. I imagined myself designing customized fitness programs that take into account the unique physical, psychological, and personal situations of a variety of individuals and groups, with clients who were excited about the empowering benefits of exercise and inspired to achieve their personal best. I aspired to be a member of a well-respected profession in which all practitioners perform their duties with the degree of skill and competence expected of health professionals, providing the finest quality service to their clients with enthusiasm and care.

A Worst-Case Scenario

Sometime after I started my business and spent less time daydreaming and more time in the world, I gradually discovered that my dream, while certainly possible for me to achieve, was at variance with the reality of my profession. This story, told to me by a young woman I know, illustrates the point. A client went to a health club for her first (and last, as it turned out) workout with a personal trainer. She tingled with excitement as she prepared to meet with her personal trainer for the first time. Even though she had been going to the health club for some time, she envisioned working with a professional personal trainer as the key to kicking her program into high gear and achieving that lean, sculpted look that entices most people into exercise in the first place. "This will be the way to get skinny," she thought gleefully. Leaving aside whether you think getting

"skinny" is a laudable goal, you'll probably agree that it's preferable to thinking "This will be the way to end up in the emergency room." Her trainer was the club's manager and claimed to have a college degree in kinesiology. He looked the part, fit and lean with an enthusiastic manner. Not only that, he was a man with a plan. The primary objective for the workout—no, the be-all and end-all of this *first session*—was to keep her heart rate elevated, even during the resistance portion. Yes, he said, you will get dizzy. Yes, you will be winded. That's how we know you're getting a quality workout, he explained.

How did he plan to accomplish this quickened pulse and increased respiration? He decided that she should run. Not walk briskly, but flat-out, heart-pounding, sweat-pouring run through the club, dodging pieces of equipment and her fellow fitness enthusiasts.

They began the workout/obstacle course. In short order, it was obvious that this workout would not disappoint. Within only a few minutes, she was winded, weak, and woozy. Her arms had turned to quivering jelly. He kept exhorting her to go faster, all the while saying, "Look at me, don't look down!" She followed his instructions well, so well that she didn't notice the small platform around one machine until she was sprawled on the floor with her face resting on it. She had tripped and turned her ankle. She fell forward and tried to brace herself with her now useless, exhausted arms, which barely cushioned her slide into what can best be described as a face skate. She said, "When I asked my trainer if I was bleeding, he said he thought I had a scratch."

Her trainer's attitude could charitably be described as unconcerned. In fact, he was completely blasé, but seemed grateful that it was winter. "When you get out to your car, just put some snow on it to keep the swelling down," he said casually before sending her on her way. "What swelling? I thought it was just a scratch," she thought as she walked shakily out to her car, her weakness and vertigo increasing with every step.

Somehow she was able to drive herself home. She stumbled into the house and lay down, hoping that soon she would feel, if not normal, at least well enough to sit up. Several hours later, she faced the fact that she had endured something more than a "scratch." She noted, "When I got to the emergency room, the staff informed me that I was lucky to have just a broken nose. They thought I had broken my cheekbone, too." Her trainer's reaction? He never even called to see if she was OK. In fact, she never heard from him again. (Her lawyer, however, did have several opportunities to talk to him and to the owners of the club.)

Learning From Others' Mistakes

The moral of the story is that there is a very wrong way to do personal training, and that plenty of people are doing it the wrong way. This incident is an illustration of a universal truth: As important and valuable as formal education is, without experience and common sense, it doesn't qualify you to do anything.

Another lesson: Just because someone wears the uniform and looks the part doesn't mean she can actually do the job. Think of that goofy old commercial where a popular soap-opera actor hawked over-the-counter medication with the line, "I'm not a doctor, but I play one on TV." Looking fit doesn't qualify a person to design safe, effective exercise programs.

Finally, an undertaking started with poorly designed objectives and executed with poorly designed plans yields poor results. Raw enthusiasm and good intentions without careful thought behind them are a dangerous combination, especially where heavy objects are involved.

I hope that you take something else from this story. Remember how the client looked forward to working with a trainer? How horribly disappointed this experience must have left her. I don't think the trainer understood the emotional investment she had in this session. The client viewed his expertise, support, and encouragement as the keys to transforming her body, and therefore her life. Perhaps to him, this session that she had anxiously anticipated for days was just another hour on the job. Perhaps he had good intentions but no common sense, a potentially dangerous combination. Whatever the case, he just didn't get it.

I want you to "get it," to understand what being a professional personal trainer is all about. My vision, though a little more realistic now, remains uncompromised: I want every trainer to understand what an important job she is doing and take seriously the responsibility to uphold the high standards that elevate our professional standing among the public. I want you to be the best you can be.

Core Beliefs: A Firm Foundation

As I thought more about my vision, I realized that it had developed from a collection of values. Without these core beliefs I would not have been able to put into words what being a personal trainer should be. They are the foundation on which the vision is built, so it's important that you know something about them.

Core Belief One: A Personal Trainer Is a Health Professional

It seems so obvious, but this point is too easily lost. Exercise is a powerful therapy. Administered correctly, it can dramatically improve most of the major indicators of good health (heart rate, blood pressure, endurance, strength, body composition). Conversely, administered incorrectly or negligently, exercise can be downright dangerous! A professional personal trainer must have a working knowledge of anatomy, physiology, and biomechanics so that he will know how to deal with each client's particular needs and limitations. How should you modify a shoulder press so your client can do it without pain? Should she be doing a shoulder press at all? How should the program of a 60-year-old diabetic differ from the program of a 30-year-old recreational athlete? Are there exercises that no one should do under any circumstances, or that this particular client shouldn't do? A professional personal trainer must be able to answer these questions.

Core Belief Two: Like All Other Fitness Professionals, Personal Trainers Are in a Position of Trust and Responsibility

We do a very important job, and therefore have a responsibility to do our work with professionalism rather than just go through the motions. We help people transform themselves from weak supplicants of whatever cards life deals them ("I used to like to work in my garden, but now my back hurts whenever I do") to fully functional, vigorous creatures who are in command of their own lives and excited about every new day and new possibility. Because we often detect silent diseases such as high blood pressure through our monitoring and screening, we are sometimes a person's first introduction to needed medical attention. This responsibility is of the utmost importance.

Perhaps it is because of the seriousness with which I regard this issue that I am astounded by the attitude of many in the fitness field. I don't mean the many fine, conscientious trainers who have great credentials and attitudes. I also don't mean you. The very fact that you're reading this book demonstrates that you have the commitment to be the best that separates you from the people I'm about to describe. I mean people like club owners who pay fit but unqualified people $6 an hour and call them "trainers." Or the muscular guy who's lifted weights for 12 years and has 20-inch biceps, but doesn't know a rotator cuff from a pant cuff.

As a personal trainer, you are in a position to have a dramatic, lifelong impact on the health of your clients. If you do a good job, your clients will be eternally grateful, and they will show it. As a person with the ability to profoundly change people's lives, you are in a unique position of trust and responsibility. Your clients will take your advice and suggestions very seriously. They will tell you personal things about their lives, their hopes, their dreams. They will let you see their real feelings, not just the happy public face that they put on the rest of the day. You must be worthy of their trust.

Core Belief Three: A Personal Trainer Is a Teacher

Recently, a client, knowing about my passion for rubber stamps, gave me one for my collection. It says "To Teach Is to Touch Someone's Life Forever." At first I was confused. Why is this for me? I haven't stood at a chalkboard since I completed the required semester of teaching in my master's program, and to this day I have trouble operating an overhead projector. Then it hit me. Of course, a personal trainer must, in addition to all other roles, be a teacher. Our overall objective must be independence for our clients. We must empower them so that they are confident enough to exercise on their own, not just when we're cracking the whip behind them. To paraphrase an old saying, "Give a man a dumbbell and you work him for a day; teach him to train and you make him fit for a lifetime." It's not enough to just show your clients how to do their workouts

correctly while you're there watching them. You have to teach them and help them master the important form points of each exercise, the things you look for when you watch them, the fine adjustments that you make to improve the effectiveness of the workout.

Core Belief Four: Any Important Endeavor Must Begin With Agreed-Upon, Specific Goals and Objectives

Everything in life, including exercise, should be about goals and objectives. Your programs, from the selection of each exercise, to the number of sets and repetitions, to the overall yearly plan for each client, should be designed with specific short-term, intermediate, and long-term objectives in mind. Similarly, you should understand the specific objective of each exercise you recommend. What muscles or muscle groups are you trying to work? Why? Making these decisions requires a lot of thought. Think back to the broken nose story. That was a great, albeit extreme, example of a poorly formulated objective leading to a really bad result. The law of unintended consequences strikes again.

Goals are more specific than general objectives. They provide landmarks on your client's journey to reaching her ultimate objective. As important as they are, designing a program with specific short-term, intermediate, and long-term goals is only the first part of the process. You've got to get your client to buy into the plan. If you can convince her that there is a logical thought process and sound planning behind what you're asking her to do, you'll have a much better chance of getting her to stick to the program over the long run. Specific, measurable, agreed-upon goals plus commitment to the process equals results!

A final, but very significant point about the importance of goals and objectives: One of the most important things you will do for your clients is to encourage and motivate them, especially during times when they are experiencing plateaus, injuries, or other periods when they don't see any progress. During these times, your job is to encourage your client to keep his eyes on the prize and remember why it's important to work out consistently and stick to a healthy diet. You must be the voice that answers the question "What's the point?" when his enthusiasm for the program flags by reminding him about his overall goals and how terrific he will feel when he achieves them. In short, motivation comes from mutual understanding and agreement about agreed-upon long- and short-term objectives. You must be able to explain the objective of every exercise, every set, and every rep you ask your client to do. Here's something really cool to think about: After your client has worked with you a while, he will actually hear your voice inside his head, encouraging him, telling him how to do it right. Think about that—it's almost like immortality.

Core Belief Five: Never Run From the Truth

Recently, one of those horror-story-of-the-night network television magazine shows featured a piece on the overprescription of antibiotics. They did the usual ambush, hidden-camera thing that has become a TV cliché. A producer visited several doctors' offices, feigning flu-like symptoms and requesting antibiotics. Two out of three of the doctors wrote prescriptions for antibiotics, even though these drugs are worthless against viruses. The next day the reporter returned to the office of one of the prescribing physicians to ask her why she would give a patient who wasn't even sick a prescription that would have no effect even if she were. The doctor explained that it wasn't her fault that patients demand antibiotics, and besides, "Medicine is a business and if I don't give them what they want they'll go somewhere else." This attitude reflects a shirking of professional responsibility that you should avoid at all costs.

Even if ethics aren't enough to convince you, here's another reason. The doctor couldn't be more wrong: This kind of thinking isn't good for business. The day will come when you have to tell a client something she doesn't want to hear. Let's face it—we'd all like to be told "Nah, you don't need to stop eating hot fudge sundaes and french fries four or five times a day. You can eat what you want and still have a body like a Sports Illustrated swimsuit model. Exercise? Only when you feel like it." No, you aren't the food police, but you are going to have to tell your clients that, if they want to achieve their goals, there are certain foods and beverages that they need to consume only in moderation, if not eliminate.

Furthermore, there are going to be days when they are going to have to push themselves (with your help, of course) to get their workouts in even when they'd rather be watching TV. You, like the doctor, may think that such frankness is no way to win friends and influence people. You may be especially reluctant to say these things to someone who is paying you. Trust me—your clients will respect you for telling them the truth. They know that they can't reach their goals without enduring a little D & D (discomfort and deprivation), and they don't really expect you to say anything different. In fact, they'd be horribly disappointed if you spared them the challenges you have planned for them. You can't blame them for trying, though.

Core Belief Six: They Say the Devil Is in the Details, but That's Not All You'll Find There

In my six-plus years of personal training, I have observed that something else is also in the details: the difference between excellence and mediocrity, between achievement and failure, between progress and stagnation. Being professional means more than the obvious things like looking the part, showing up on time, and not dropping a dumbbell on the client's foot. The differences between the qualified health professional and the glorified spotter might not be obvious at first glance. They might even be invisible, but the difference in the effect on clients is anything but. It is dramatic. Your background in anatomy and physiology, not to mention your knowledge and understanding of your client's unique needs, marks you for all the world as a caring, knowledgeable professional. Your attentiveness to every detail, and especially to your client, distinguishes you from the casual hit-or-miss gym rat providing an occassional tip or spot, or the distracted club employee who may be called away at any moment to answer a phone or help someone at the counter.

Core Belief Seven: Individuals Have More Control Over Their Health Than a Health Professional

We have a responsibility to educate our clients about how much control they have over their own health and independence. Many of us have accepted as inevitable the loss of strength and independence that people often suffer as they get older, but we know now that our bodies don't have to tumble into an accelerating decline, if we are prepared to do something about it. With your help, your client will realize the control he has over his own health, and this feeling of power and positive energy will carry over into every aspect of life.

Core Belief Eight: A Business, No Matter How Small, Should Be Run Like a Business

Some trainers seem to believe that because they are one-person businesses (or maybe because they don't have to wear suits, nylons, and dress shoes to work) they are somehow exempt from all the irritating paperwork that torments other small business people. To remain clueless about these things is not only unprofessional, it's risky.

Taxes aren't the only thing to worry about. Potential liability for injuries is a serious issue for personal trainers, whether they realize it or not. It's ironic that the trainer most likely to injure someone is least likely to have any insurance or any assets to compensate the victims of his negligence. Even though the best protection is careful planning and program design, a practicing health professional should maintain adequate insurance coverage and provide his clients with informed consents and waivers to sign prior to beginning a program.

The Moral of the Story

Recently, I received a note from a longtime client. In part, she wrote, "As one gets older, it is too easy to accept and believe in a lot of self-imposed limitations. I was fortunate enough to meet you before much damage was done. You have a unique and nurturing approach that I'm sure is natural, not cultivated. It stems from a high degree of intelligence, sensitivity, and generosity. Simply stated, thanks to me for finding you. Thanks to you for being there." My vision for you is to receive notes like this from your many satisfied clients and to glow with satisfaction and pride the way I am as I write these words and relive the feeling I had when I read that note.

PART I

ESTABLISHING YOUR PERSONAL TRAINING BUSINESS

CHAPTER 1

Standing on the Threshold

You're considering a career in personal training. Now what?

Some Bad Reasons to Become a Personal Trainer

- You're really muscular and have a great tan
- You like to hang around the gym all the time anyway
- You like to boss people around, and to get paid for it would be a dream come true
- You like to wear spandex
- It's a great way to meet chicks
- It's a great way to meet guys
- You got fired from the convenience market
- All of the other jobs you qualify for pay minimum wage
- You've been lifting weights for 12 years and have 22-inch arms
- You hated school and don't want to go back

 Threshold Question 1: *Is It Right for Me?*

In every career there are trade-offs, and personal training is no exception. The question you have to answer is whether the trade-offs add up to a good deal for you.

If you're having trouble deciding whether to become a personal trainer, think about this:

If you decide to take the plunge and strike out on your own, I guarantee there will be a beautiful, clear day when you are cruising along in your car, clad in brightly colored spandex, liberated from the business attire that binds so many of your friends, listening to tunes in the middle of the day rather than the annoying babble of office gossip, bathed in sunshine rather than complexion-sallowing fluorescent light, wondering what took you so long to decide to become a personal trainer.

The Bad Part

Despite what you may be tempted to think when you listen to your friends describe their glamorous, high-paying gigs, there is no perfect occupation, and personal training is no exception.

Scheduling Problems

When you're a personal trainer, you have days like this: You have a 6:45 a.m. workout at Client A's home, and a 10:30 a.m. workout at Client B's house, which is 10 minutes from Client A's. The only problem is that you have a 9:00 a.m. workout at Client C's club, which is 30 minutes away from Client A's and Client B's! Argh!

Unfortunately, despite your efforts to make sure that you schedule appointments close to each other to avoid nonstop road running, sometimes it will be unavoidable. Also, clients sometimes need to change their regular appointments because of changes in their schedules. You must try to accommodate them, but also try to structure your regular schedule so that such deviations are the exception and not the rule. The juggling act isn't easy, but it does get easier after you've established your clientele. In the beginning, it's really tempting to take any client you think you can help, no matter how far away.

An important word to the wise: Resist the desire to fill every waking moment with client sessions. You must include time for planning, preparing workouts, and doing administrative work. I suggest that you plan one hour of office work for every client session you schedule. In addition, be sure to schedule free time into your week. Burnout is a real risk for personal trainers! If you don't recharge your batteries on a regular basis, you will find yourself going through the motions, conducting workouts like a robot and losing your edge. Avoid this danger by planning ahead!

Travel Isn't Always Fun

Many personal trainers work in some combination of clubs and homes and therefore spend a fairly large portion of the day traveling. (Yes, you need a reliable car.) While travel is inevitable under these circumstances, do anything you can to avoid excessive travel. Not only does it wear you out, it limits the number of hours you can work with clients. If you can't stand the idea of traveling a lot, consider a personal training job in a club.

Not Enough Hours in the Day

Speaking of hours, they won't be 9 to 5 in this gig. The reasons should be obvious. Most of the people you will be working with have jobs or other commitments and can't work out in the middle of the day. You will probably work what is effectively a split shift—three or four sessions in the morning and another three or four in the evening.

It's Many Jobs Rolled Into One

When you work for yourself, you have to wear many hats—manager, bookkeeper, and secretary as well as service provider. You need to decide whether you want to assume the responsibility of your own business. If you enjoy working with clients, but would prefer not dealing with administrative responsibilities, consider strongly whether you should be in business for yourself. You may be better suited to working as an employee in a club.

Lugging the Equipment

It's not only enduring those long and irregular hours that will leave you feeling like you've been pulled through a keyhole at the end of some days. Between carrying a heavy bag full of equipment from house to house and demonstrating exercises, you will learn what seems obvious: Personal training is a physical job!

The Good Part

While some personal trainers work in a health club setting as employees, this book is written for those of you who are more entrepreneurial. If you currently work in a club and are frustrated by some of the limitations imposed by the need to see a minimum number of clients in a day or by management restrictions on how you design your programs, you should consider striking out on your own. Having your own business has tremendous rewards that make all the hard work worth it for many. You will be able to provide better, more personalized service, and you will be able to use your knowledge and skill to design innovative programs for your clients.

Flexible Hours

Irregular hours are also flexible hours—time in the middle of the day to do other things like your grocery shopping, buying stamps, your own workout. All of these things can be done at times when most other people are working, a definite advantage.

Creative and Expressive Freedom

One of the most rewarding things about doing personal training is the opportunity to help individual clients set goals and reach them. Each client is a new opportunity to apply your knowledge and skill to reach a desired result.

Fulfilling Professional Relationships

My clients are the greatest people who have ever walked the face of the earth (and I'm not just saying that because I know many of them are reading this). They think I've changed their lives, but it's really the other way around; they've changed my life. I draw inspiration from their determination. I look forward to hearing about all the interesting things they're doing. I feel fortunate to run ideas by them and get their advice. It's a mutual admiration society, which shouldn't be surprising. When you help someone achieve something as significant and life-changing as becoming fit, watching her transform not only her body but her attitude, you become a part of that transformation. And the really amazing thing is that it transforms you, too.

 ## Threshold Question 2: *What Do I Need to Get Started?*

After you've figured out whether personal training is right for you, the next questions you need to ask yourself are about your own readiness. You may need more training, and that might affect your decision to go ahead with starting your own personal training business.

Do I Need a Degree?

A degree is like a computer. No, you don't *need* one, in the sense that you can get by in life and in business without it; however, you'll get a lot farther with it. Let me explain. Suppose a potential client wants to hire Joe Muscleman to train him. Joe barely made it through high school, and will never be mistaken for Albert Einstein's long-lost twin brother. What's wrong with this picture? From a legal and regulatory standpoint, nothing. At least for the present time, personal training is a self-regulated industry. Consumers are free to hire anyone they want, and service providers don't need any credentials.

That's theory, here's reality: Both individual clients and managers at quality clubs who hire personal trainers tend to be well-educated, and many of them understand what qualifications and educational background they should demand in a personal trainer. Surveys have shown that fewer than half (in some surveys, fewer than 25 percent) of personal trainers surveyed have earned a degree in a fitness field. But because most clients looking for a personal trainer have degrees, they will choose a degreed trainer almost every time, even if it costs them more money.

I suggest that you acquire at least a bachelor's degree in exercise physiology, exercise science, physical education, or some related field. If you don't have a degree yet, begin taking classes. Some colleges and universities have special programs for fitness enthusiasts looking at careers in personal training. Courses in anatomy and physiology, nutrition, exercise physiology, and related subjects will be invaluable to you, and potential clients are much more likely to become actual clients if you have

taken such classes. You will be able to pursue your career as a personal trainer and get clients while you're in school, provided that you get certified by a reputable organization.

Do I Need a Certification?

Unlike a degree, which is still at least officially an optional requirement, certification is essential. For one thing, the overwhelming majority of personal trainers are certified. If you aren't, you'll come up way short by comparison. Second, you will find it impossible to get liability insurance without certification.

Reasons to Get Certified by One of the Top Programs
• Your professional credibility will be enhanced
• You will learn something while preparing for the exam
• You will be able to get liability insurance through the organization
• You will be able to get referrals from physicians and other health professionals

Flip to the back of any bodybuilding magazine, past the photographs of the massive, tanned hulks with the bikini-clad admirers draped across their massive chests, and page through the ads. No doubt you'll see several certification program advertisements, some of which require nothing more than writing a check and completing a home study program. You might be tempted to write said check and get started tomorrow. That seems like a lot less hassle than one of these highfalutin programs that make you get a degree and take a written (and maybe even a practical) exam. So you might reasonably ask, "Does it matter which certification I get?"

The short answer: Yes. There are over 271 certification programs in the fitness field. (At least there were as of this writing. By the time you read this, there will probably be more, since new ones seem to appear daily.) They range from programs that require passing a written and practical exam (the American College of Sports Medicine, or ACSM) to those that require only that you pay a fee (usually hefty) and attend a weekend seminar. I know of at least one program founded for the sole reason that existing certification programs like ACSM's set such high standards and have such "extremely clinical" education materials. They make no bones about the fact that they want to set the bar low enough so that anyone who can fog a mirror can make it over! These substandard programs are tempting because some of them permit a great deal of flexibility in not only their requirements, but also the dates and times you can take their tests. As previously mentioned, some even permit home study and testing.

Before you write your check, though, consider this: Fitness consumers are beginning to understand the differences among the various certification programs, so you should aim high and get the best certification you can. Your decision about certification will affect whether you will get referrals from other health professionals and whether you can get access to clubs and gyms. If anyone can just pay the fee and get the organization's certificate, is it really worth anything? What sort of reputation does this certification have? Does it have high standards? How long has the program been in business? Will you be able to get liability insurance with this certification?

The ACSM certification is the gold standard in the field. I highly recommend it. The American Council on Exercise (ACE, the most widely held certification), the Aerobics and Fitness Association of America (AFAA), the National Dance-Exercise Instructors Training Association (NDEITA), and the

Aerobics and Fitness Association of America (AFAA)
15250 Ventura Blvd., Suite 200
Sherman Oaks, CA 91403
818-905-0040 or 800-446-2322

American College of Sport Medicine (ACSM)
P.O. Box 1440
Indianapolis, IN 46206-1440
317-637-9200

American Council on Exercise (ACE—formerly IDEA)
5820 Oberlin Dr., Suite 102
San Diego, CA 92121
800-825-3636

National Dance-Exercise Instructors Training Association (NDEITA)
1503 South Washington Avenue, Suite 208
Minneapolis, MN 55454-1037
612-340-1306

National Strength and Conditioning Association (NSCA)
P.O. Box 38909
Colorado Springs, CO 80937
719-632-6722 or 402-476-6669

National Strength and Conditioning Association (NSCA) certifications are also highly regarded. Don't waste as much as several hundred dollars on a substandard certification. Make the effort and go the extra mile. Get certified by ACSM, ACE, AFAA, NDEITA, or NSCA. You will be glad you did, and so will your clients.

Do I Need a License?

Sometimes it seems as if anyone can claim to be a personal trainer—the muscular bagboy who helps out at a friend's gym in his spare time, the housewife veteran of countless aerobics classes. The reason it seems that way is that, theoretically at least, it's true: Anyone can! Personal training is a self-regulated industry, and any individual can claim to be a personal trainer, qualified or not.

While several states have considered requiring licenses for fitness instructors and personal trainers, none have enacted such regulations. (However, Louisiana recently enacted a license requirement for clinical exercise physiologists, those who work in cardiac rehabilitation programs under the supervision of physicians.)

While you may be relieved that you don't need a license, you should know that many potential clients have serious concerns about the competence of personal trainers, and they will be looking for evidence that you are more than a friendly personality and a hard body. They are likely to look to your academic background, experience, and certification.

Do I Need CPR Training?

CPR is like your local fire department or the Maytag repairman—you hope you never have to call them, but you're awfully glad they're there if you do. Speaking of your local fire department, they sometimes offer CPR classes. You can also get your CPR card by attending a class and passing a test at your local YMCA or American Red Cross chapter. Be sure to do so well in advance of the deadline for sending in your certification exam registration. You will need to send a copy of your CPR card along with your exam registration form.

It is absolutely necessary that you obtain and maintain current CPR certification. Aside from the remote possibility that you will actually have to use your lifesaving skills, most certification programs require that you have a current, valid CPR certification in order to register for the exam. The legal standard in most U.S. communities dictates that a reasonable and prudent personal trainer will have a current CPR certification, and your liability insurance carrier may ask for proof of your compliance with this requirement. Unquestionably, if you ever find yourself in a position where your legal status matters, it will be significantly weaker if you don't maintain current CPR certification.

Threshold Question 3: Do I Have What It Takes?

You've got a degree, and you're certified by ACSM. Your knowledge of anatomy, physiology, biomechanics, and nutrition is first rate. Is this enough? Unfortunately, it isn't. To move into the upper echelon of professional personal trainers, you also need superior communication skills and a personal commitment to fitness.

Superior Communication Skills

A personal trainer must be able to explain and clarify, simplify the complex, and focus the client's attention on making that all-important mind-muscle connection. It's more than just breaking down biomechanical technicalities.

Contrary to popular belief and practice, listening is the biggest part of communication. Your function is not to demonstrate how much you know by controlling and dominating the session, filling it with a nonstop lecture. You are there to help your client reach his goals, and you need to adapt to his needs and wants. Listen and be flexible to create the most effective and enjoyable personal training experience possible.

"God gave us two ears and one mouth for a reason." Ancient proverb

---

Words mean things, usually different things to different people. Choose them carefully, and tailor them to your client. Your goal is to make yourself understood. Using anatomical and scientific words may be appropriate in some contexts. I have clients who are physicians, nurses, and chiropractors. With these clients, it is not only appropriate, it is more understandable to say "iliac crest" rather than "hip bone." On the other hand, a novice exerciser who has no background in anatomy is likely to think the iliac crest is something you encountered on your last

ski vacation. One of your goals should be to educate your client about her body. Eventually your client's anatomical vocabulary should improve enough to know some of the most commonly used body landmarks. During your first few months together, she will have more than enough to remember. Keep this in mind when deciding which words to use and when.

Don't forget the role of nonverbal communication. Do you arrive at your session looking like you've lost three nights of sleep, your wallet, and your last friend, round-shouldered and head-hanging? What message does your posture convey? Tired, low-energy, zero enthusiasm? Ask yourself— would you want to work out coached by you?

Personal Commitment to Fitness

A friend of mine recently attended a workshop on parenting. As she listened to the lecturer sharing her insights about how to get children to behave, a thought occurred to her. She raised her hand and asked, "How many children do you have?" The young woman seemed a little flustered, and said hesitatingly, "Well, none." Needless to say, that revelation affected her credibility like a needle affects a helium balloon. The audience's attention drifted from the speaker's words to football standings, TV sitcoms, and similar topics of greater seriousness. Like most intelligent adults today, they had little patience listening to someone who has never done something tell other people how to do it.

"Do as I say, not as I do" may work for some parents (not many, I suspect), but without genuine passion and commitment, you will not be an effective fitness coach. A successful personal trainer must have a personal commitment to fitness. He must feel passionate about what exercise can do for the body, the mind, and the spirit. He must infect his client with this passion so that the client feels it, too. Going through the motions won't cut it for you or your clients. You will lose your tolerance for the challenges inherent in a personal trainer's day. Soon you will lose your clients.

"The difference between the right word and the almost right word is the difference between the lightning and the lightning bug." Mark Twain

---

Approach personal training with alacrity and commitment, and watch your satisfied client base grow!

CHAPTER 2

Business and Legal Matters

The following text is provided for general informational purposes only. Every individual's situation is different, and your personal situation might require the attention of an attorney licensed to practice in your state. This information is no substitute for the personal advice of knowledgeable advisors (a licensed attorney, a good accountant) who have reviewed your situation. When you're deciding whether to incorporate, what to do about your tax situation, or a similar important matter, do yourself a favor—get a good lawyer and an honest accountant!

Questions and Answers

Still, there are some general rules of thumb to creating a good business. Keep both your goals and limitations in mind as you answer the following questions.

Do I Need to Incorporate?

In my opinion, most personal trainers beginning a new business do not need to be concerned about incorporating. The main reason to incorporate is to attempt to shield yourself from personal liability. I suspect that this is less of a concern for you than for some businesses because

- you are doing everything you can to avoid potential liability,
- you have not worked with any clients prior to making sure that your liability insurance is in force, and
- since you are the entire business, if you do injure someone, you'll likely be called to account,

corporation or not. (This is what lawyers like to call "piercing the corporate veil.")

If your business expands and you hire one or more employees, you should discuss incorporating with your attorney and accountant.

How Much Should I Charge?

In a free market, you should set your rates by checking out the rates for similar services in your area. (As of this writing, there is a broad range of fees charged by personal trainers, anywhere from $20 to $100 per session.) What do other trainers with similar qualifications charge for their services? The key there is "similar qualifications." There may be "trainers" with no educational background, certification, or experience working in clubs, but if you have a master's degree in exercise physiology, are certified by ACSM, and have years of practical experience, you're in a different league. Let's face it: You didn't spend all that time and effort getting your degree to earn less than the typical street musician. Unless you're independently wealthy and

Factors to Consider When Setting Your Rates
• Your education
• Your experience
• Your geographic location
• Rates charged by other personal trainers in your area
• The length of your sessions
• The location of your sessions

you want to do personal training for your own enjoyment, you need to get paid what you're worth.

The converse is true: If you've been lifting weights for 10 years but have no educational background, no degree, and no certification, it's not realistic to expect to get paid top dollar. Investigate the market. Find out what other trainers in your area with similar qualifications are charging and use your good judgment. You might be tempted to undercut the competition when you're getting started. Think twice before using this approach. You will probably end up with a booked schedule, but you'll be bringing in substantially fewer dollars than the market says you're worth. It's only a matter of time before you'll have to raise your prices, which means you'll have to present all your clients with a rate increase.

Most trainers' sessions last approximately one hour, and the suggestions about billing I'm making here are based on the assumption that your sessions will last that long. Once you determine your hourly fee, you'll have a basis for deciding how much to charge for shorter sessions, if you decide you want to do them. For example, you might decide to offer half-hour sessions to address individual client needs, such as learning sport-specific exercises or for "checkups" with clients you've taught a routine and who have been working out on their own for a while.

> Decide whether you're going to bill your clients monthly, per session, or in some other way. Will your charge per session be the same no matter how many sessions a client signs up for, or will you offer package deals? Will you bill clients for cancelled sessions? If so, under what circumstances? Whatever you decide, decide *now*!

Another factor to consider is travel time. Sometimes you will decide to work with a client outside your usual geographical service area. If you do, you should consider billing at least some part of your hourly fee as travel time. Let's face it: In your business, your time is your stock and trade.

Decide carefully your rates and methods of billing. You need to have a policy so you can respond to potential clients. Imagine this: You're sitting around one day waiting for the phone to ring, hoping it's a potential client, when it actually does! You and the person have a very pleasant conversation, during which you explain all your wonderful qualifications and all the miraculous things you can do for him, and he seems very interested in hiring you. Before it's a done deal, he just needs to know the answer to one question: "How much is this going to cost me?"

You've got to be able to answer that, and fast, otherwise your prospect will be an ex-prospect before you can say "Body by Jake."

Bookkeeping and Financial Records

I cannot overemphasize the importance of keeping accurate records of dollars in and dollars out. As soon as you have established your business (ordered your business cards, gotten your liability insurance in place, etc.), and before you accept a single client, open a separate checking account for the business. You should do this even if you aren't incorporated and even if you have only one or two clients. You're probably thinking, "Oh, that's not important. I'm not making that much. My clients all pay cash. Who's going to know?" Wrong. There are a couple of reasons that this is a bad idea. First, remember that when it comes to income, we're all dealing with the reality of taxes and laws. If your income and the taxes paid on it are placed under IRS scrutiny, you must be able to prove that you have paid all state and federal taxes due on what you earned. If you can't, you will owe not only the back taxes as calculated by the IRS, but also interest and penalties. When totaled up, this will probably be a number larger than you have ever seen in connection with your name and a dollar sign.

Now imagine what a mess you'll have on your hands if you haven't kept the money you collect from your clients separate from what you got from Aunt Tillie on your last birthday, and the paycheck you got working in the retail store for two weeks before Christmas. Also, depending on how you bill your clients, you might be asked whether a client received credit for a missed session, or some similar question about payments or amounts due. You must be able to respond to these inquiries as a professional. If you can't produce good records, you will probably be forced to eat the cost of missed sessions, even if the client really isn't entitled to credit.

> Trust me: If you don't keep good accounting records, you will regret it!

You can set up your books either manually or on a computer. I highly recommend the latter. Using a computer simplifies the process of figuring out income and expenses for tax purposes at the end of the year. Here's the method I use, which has been quite successful for me. At the beginning of the month, bill your clients for the month's sessions in advance. Prepare the invoices on your computer, using either your bookkeeping program or a separate database program. Keep track of each client's sessions in your appointment book, and at the end of the month, before sending out the next month's invoices, figure out whether any credits for missed or canceled sessions are due. Compute the amount due for the upcoming month. This is the amount for next month's invoice.

Most small business owners keep their books on a cash basis, as opposed to using the accrual method of accounting. With the former method, you record income when you receive it and expenses when you pay them. Your accountant can help you set up your books. Your business is small enough that once you get some help setting them up, you should be able to keep the books yourself.

What About Taxes?

Each individual's income tax liability is dictated by that individual's specific situation. (Married? Single? Children? Homeowner? Renter? The considerations are endless.) The important thing is, as mentioned above, the last thing you want is the IRS breathing down your neck! You should consult an accountant or other professional tax advisor about your specific tax situation. A couple of things to think about:

- If you earn income and you are not an employee who has taxes withheld, you will need to pay estimated quarterly taxes, estimates of the amount of the taxes you will owe when you file your annual return.

- If you do personal training as a second job, or if you do personal training part-time as an employee of a club and the rest of the time as an entrepreneur, do not assume that because you have taxes withheld at your job, you don't have to pay estimated quarterly taxes. The amount of your withholding at your job covers the wages that you earn at that job. It does not take into account additional amounts you might earn moonlighting. If you should pay estimated taxes, but don't, you may owe penalties and interest in amounts that will make you seriously regret ignoring this little detail.

- If you have decided to incorporate your business as a C corporation (as opposed to a subchapter S corporation—ask your lawyer or accountant to explain), your corporation may owe corporate taxes separate from individual income taxes.

- As a service business with only one employee (yourself), you probably won't have to pay sales taxes, since most localities don't tax services. (I say "probably," but I don't know your state and local law. If you aren't absolutely positive about your local laws and regulations, find someone who is and ask!) You will, however, need to pay payroll taxes on the salary that the business pays you. Your tax advisor can help you through the mechanics of computing the amount of the payroll tax and making the payroll tax deposit.

Licensing and Other Burdensome Governmental Requirements

In addition to taxes, your state, county, or municipality might impose additional obligations on you and your business, such as business franchise taxes, or, if you sell products, sales taxes. In addition, some jurisdictions require that businesses file a fictitious name certificate, a document stating that, for example, Hard as a Rock Personal Training is owned by Sally Jones, an individual, or, if the business is incorporated, by SJ, Inc., a corporation doing business as Hard as a Rock Personal Training. If you don't understand these things backward and forward yourself (and most of us don't), do yourself a favor—consult a competent advisor.

Legal Matters

Many personal trainers have never stopped to think about the fact that a lawsuit could be filed against them, and are downright terrified when they discover this. It's an unfortunate fact that we live in an extremely litigious society, and anyone can sue anyone. We all heard about the woman who spilled hot coffee in her lap and then sued McDonald's. The courts are filled with other outrageous examples of careless, silly people trying to avoid responsibility for their own actions and achieve victim status and the consequent dollar payoff. Is it inevitable that you will face a lawsuit? No, I don't think the picture for personal trainers is that bleak. While it's true that exercise is not without risk and injuries do happen sometimes no matter how careful we are, you shouldn't lie awake at night worrying about getting sued.

The best protection against lawsuits is to avoid problems by screening your clients; designing safe, effective programs; and exercising care while working with your clients. If you are sued despite doing these things, you will be way ahead of the game if you have a degree and are certified by one of the nationally recognized organizations (see chapter 1). You can also strengthen your credentials by taking continuing education classes, something most of the certifying bodies require for you to maintain your certification. If you consistently follow specific procedures for handling equipment, you minimize the risk of making a mistake.

Finally, remember that the personal trainer-client relationship is first and foremost just that: a personal relationship. If you show genuine concern for your client's needs, desires, and well-being and you really do relate to clients as individuals, your chances of being sued are greatly diminished. Concern for your client is more than showing genuine warm feelings. It is also performing your job as a professional and exercising care to avoid any potential harm to your clients. Read on.

Torts, Liability, and Other Scary Legal Words

Tort is one of those words that you probably can't define unless you attended law school. The study of torts is part of the core curriculum in every law school in the common law world. That notwithstanding, it has been said that a really satisfactory definition of the word has never been found. Leave it to the law professors and legal theoreticians to worry about semantical abstractions. Here is a workable definition of *tort*: A tort is an act or a failure to act that violates a legally created right and allows the injured party to sue for damages or injunctive relief; that is, it gives rise to liability. For the personal trainer, a tort means causing an injury to your client, which is usually physical, but could be emotional.

Liability—what is it, and why should you care? Being liable means being legally responsible for the consequences of one's actions or omissions. If your actions result in injury or loss to someone, have you committed a tort and subjected yourself to liability? You have if the following elements are met:

- Duty: You have an obligation to do or refrain from doing something
- Breach: You do not live up to this obligation
- Proximate cause: Your act or omission causes the injury
- Damages: Someone is injured as a result of your act or omission

---

Taking Care

In the context of being a personal trainer, what does this mean to you? When you work with your client, you have an obligation to use ordinary care to refrain from causing injury. *Ordinary care* means that your actions are consistent with those of a reasonable, prudent personal trainer. This is a way of referring to the legal concept of the "standard of care." If you are ever hauled into court to answer for allegedly injuring a client, and your state does not require trainers to be licensed, you will probably be judged by a standard of care based on

- the standards set by the leading national certifying organizations, and
- expert witness testimony about what a careful personal trainer would have done in the same situation.

Instruction and Supervision

As a one-on-one trainer, you are responsible for providing proper instruction and supervision. So what exactly does that mean? Glad you asked. It means:

- Individualized and continuous instruction. To do this properly, you must stay in close physical proximity to your client with all of your attention focused on her.
- Accurate instruction. This means ensuring correct form and technique on every exercise and paying attention to proper body mechanics on every exercise.
- Supervision. This means executing proper spotting technique and giving attention to things that could cause an unsafe situation in the workout area or with your client herself, such as not wearing a belt during squats.

Recommending Equipment

You'll get a lot of questions from your clients about what type of equipment to buy. The rule here is not to recommend anything without knowing the reason for your recommendation and being able to document it. If you aren't sure about a piece of equipment, say so, but try to help your client by recommending a good fitness equipment retailer where he can go and discuss the right product for him. Notice I said a *good* fitness equipment retailer. I don't mean some cavernous 100,000-square-foot sports superstore where customers can be seen wandering aimlessly through the aisles and a knowledgeable employee is rarer than a snowstorm in Maui. Once you've decided to do personal training, build a relationship with a quality retailer. Go into the retailer's establishment. Introduce yourself. Ask whether you can leave some of your cards. When you get an equipment inquiry, suggest that your client go to this retailer, and be sure he mentions your name.

Handling Emergencies

If you provide proper instruction and supervision, you probably won't have to deal with injuries or other emergencies, but remember that proper instruction and supervision includes proper response to emergency situations. Suppose your client drops a dumbbell on her foot. Did you make sure that your client had control of the dumbbell when you handed it to her? That is, did you say, "Do you have it?" Did you recommend that your client wear gloves when lifting weights? Were her hands sweaty from her warm-up, making them more likely to be slippery? Were you standing close by and spotting your client properly? Did you take the dumbbell when it looked like she was failing? These are the questions that are relevant to the issue of proper instruction and supervision.

If, despite your best efforts, an accident should happen, you should follow standard first aid procedures. In this example, you should make sure that your client sits down and gets off her foot. You might need to call an ambulance, depending on how serious the accident was. Do not attempt to treat injuries that are beyond your knowledge or ability. The other extremely important thing you need to do is to document exactly what happened. Immediately after you have seen to first aid matters, sit down and write a summary of the accident. Be specific! Describe the movement your client was doing, the nature of the accident, and any other details you can think of. This information could be important to your client's physician. Be especially careful to address the questions in this paragraph. If you did everything right, you'll want to have it on record.

Handling Equipment

A big part of your job as a personal trainer will involve handling equipment: machines, free weights, and other similar items. For clients who have never set foot in a gym or lifted a weight, your expertise with equipment will be one of the main reasons they retain you. Sometimes those of us who spend most of our time with these tools of the trade can get a bit complacent about them, not consciously aware of how powerful, and, if misused, how dangerous, they can be. Rest assured that if your client gets injured, such lapses in concentration can be very costly. Always remember to ask yourself, "What's the worst thing that can happen if I do this?" (or don't do this, as the case may be). The answer is the risk that you are assuming. Is it an acceptable one for you and your client?

Check and Double Check

You'd be amazed how easy it is to pick up two dumbbells of different weights and not notice the difference, especially between 15s and 20s. This is not a disaster unless you hand them to your client. He is depending on you for guidance, instruction, and support—how's it going to look if you hand him the wrong dumbbells? (And, by the way, you should hand the dumbbell to your client rather than letting him get it himself; this gives you an opportunity to make sure it isn't loose.) Before you hand the client a dumbbell, or before you allow him to begin a set on a machine, make sure you have the right dumbbells or have the pin in the right place.

Make a notation in the client's workout record form (see appendix A) of the position she uses on a particular machine. If you have to adjust a seat on a bike or machine, make sure the pin is in place by sitting on it yourself before you allow the client to sit on it. Also, pay attention to the position and condition of cables on machines. Do they look frayed? Are they off the track? Check the hooks connecting the cables to pulldown and pushdown bars. Sometimes these hooks bend due to the amount of force they have to handle in a typical gym or club. I don't hesitate to suggest that a client refrain from using a particular bar if it appears the item is nearly worn through. Make sure equipment is clean. (Some clients are more comfortable placing a towel on a bench before they lie on it, which I encourage.) In short, check everything: the equipment, its condition, and any adjustments you make before you let your client use it.

Don't Modify Equipment

Sometimes in gyms you see people using equipment in, shall we say, innovative and creative ways. There may be no problem with this sort of thing if you are not responsible for anyone else's well-being. As a professional, you must realize that a lawsuit can turn on the issue of design for particular purpose, as in, a lawnmower isn't designed to be hand held and used as a hedgeclipper. For example, the gym where

I work out has a seated horizontal bench press machine. It's clear that this machine was designed with one exercise in mind. The subject places her hands on short handles that are directly in front of her shoulders. They are not adjustable. Seeing this inflexibility as a design defect, some people attempt to correct it by placing a straight bar between the two handles so they can do a close-grip variation of the exercise. I see people do this almost every day. It should be apparent to you that this procedure might not be safe, especially with a beginner.

Remember the question: What's the worst thing that could happen? The bar could slip, fly up, and whack the client in the face. When this or any workout accident is reviewed in hindsight, what seemed like a reasonable and creative way to work a particular muscle group will usually be transformed into a clear example of trainer negligence and stupidity. In fact, it will probably seem that this was the dumbest thing that any trainer ever did. How could you do such a thing? You couldn't, you wouldn't, and you won't if you follow this simple rule: Don't modify equipment.

Free Weight Smarts

As you no doubt know, working with free weights is different than working with machines. Here are a few rules you need to follow:

1. Always use collars on bars.

2. When you hand a weight to a client, always ask "Do you have it?" and make sure that you have control of the weight until he says "Yes." Explain this rule to your clients. Tell them that until they tell you they have it, you won't let go. Never assume that the client has the weight!

3. Always be aware of other objects and people in the workout area.

4. If you approach a loaded Olympic bar on a cage-style rack, get some help stripping the plates. Don't try to pull them all off one side and then the other because if you do, the weight remaining on the bar after you've pulled it all off one side may cause the bar to flip up in the air and crash to the ground. The best thing that will happen is a very loud, embarrassing crash. I don't think you want to imagine the worst thing. This won't happen on a safety squat rack where the bar rests on an angled support.

5. You might have noticed that gyms are minefields: There are usually dumbbells, handles, barbells, and other paraphernalia on

the floor, and heavy objects are moving through the air, sometimes seemingly without guidance. Watch out! Pay strict attention to things on and off the floor. Never move in a direction without looking first. Warn your client of these hazards, too.

Proper Spotting Technique

One of your jobs during the workout is to properly spot the client. Proper spotting requires that you understand the exercise well enough to select the biomechanically efficient place to spot and have your complete attention focused on your client while he is doing the exercise. Follow these rules:

• **Preview**. Before you begin the exercise, explain to your client that you will be spotting him on the exercise just to make sure he can complete his final repetition safely. Tell him that your assistance may be in the form of applying a little help by touching the bar or dumbbells or by stabilizing a body part by applying a little direct pressure to it (the elbows, for example, during a dumbbell press). This is a good time to explain to clients, novice weightlifters especially, that you will be placing your hands on their bodies, in a purely professional way, of course. You don't want to startle someone hoisting a weight by touching him unexpectedly.

• **Communicate**. Baseball outfielders can attest to the importance of always communicating with your partner in a common enterprise. "I've got it, I've got it" is important in the gym as well as in the field. Imagine this unfortunate scenario: Your client is using a pec deck. You think "She's doing just fine controlling this weight. I don't need to keep my hands on the pads." She thinks "I can try to force out a couple more reps. She's spotting me." The client loses control of the pads and is seriously injured. All of this could have been avoided if you both were on the same page.

Don't get distracted!

I like to tell my clients in advance where I will be spotting them (elbows on a flat dumbbell press, waist on a squat, for example), and how we will proceed. ("I'll be handing you the right dumbbell first, and when we have finished this set, please lower the dumbbells and bring them down to your side. Then I'll take the left".)

Be sure that you apply equal assistance to both arms in a dumbbell exercise. Otherwise, you can throw the client off balance.

- **Focus**. A distracted spotter is worse than no spotter because he gives the lifter a false sense of security, which, if relied upon, can lead to disaster.

Remote Control

I'd like to mention other areas that raise legal issues for personal trainers, over and above the general liability matters previously discussed. For example, you might think it's a great idea to take your client out on a power walk in a remote area (and by remote, I don't mean some secluded hideaway, I mean a place other than the one in which you typically conduct workouts). What if an emergency arises in that place, where there might be no phone and no way to get help if you need to? How about taking your client out for a bike ride? These situations raise the issue of *premises liability*. If you recommend an unusual location for a workout, you have a duty to warn your client about dangers that might be present.

If you decide to do this (although it's hard to know why you would), I have four suggestions:

1. Visit the area ahead of time and investigate it for obvious dangers that you definitely want to avoid and potential problems that you want to be aware of, work around, and warn your client about.

2. Check with your insurance carrier to make sure your liability policy covers outdoor workouts.

3. Have your attorney prepare a specialized waiver or informed consent for this type of workout.

4. Finally, if I were to take a client on this sort of workout, I would take a cellular phone along just in case of an emergency. Make sure the area is on 911, or if not find out the emergency number. Write it on a card and take it with you. Better yet, tape it to the phone.

Insurance

Yes! No matter how careful you are, someone could get injured, which is why all personal trainers must have liability insurance. Not only does it identify you as a professional, liability insurance protects you if someone gets injured as a result of your actions by providing and paying for an attorney to defend you, and sometimes paying a settlement to your client. If you try to work with clients in health clubs or similar facilities, you will almost certainly have to demonstrate that you have current liability insurance by providing the management with a copy of your endorsement.

Insurance is another advantage of certification, as you can often get affordable liability insurance through your certifying organization. ACE, NSCA, and ACSM offer liability insurance, as do several other certifying organizations. However you get it, just get it! It is extremely important that you have liability insurance in force before you do any personal training. Pay close attention to the date and time that your policy becomes effective and expires.

Waivers and Informed Consents

In addition to a health history questionnaire, before you start working with a new client, you should require her to sign a waiver and informed consent. As we previously mentioned, exercise is a powerful therapy, and as such, has risks as well as benefits. The waiver and informed consent advises your client of the risks and benefits of the program and may give you some protection if a lawsuit is filed against you.

A sample waiver and informed consent is given in appendix A. Please keep in mind that liability laws differ from state to state, and so it is extremely important that you have your waiver reviewed by an attorney licensed in your state before you use it. These forms are provided for informational purposes only. They are not intended to substitute for the judgment and skill of an attorney licensed to practice in your state. Keep one thing in mind: The best waiver is one that you never have to refer to again because of your strict attention to proper safety procedures.

Appendix A contains a sample health history questionnaire as well as a sample physician's consent form. As in the case of the waiver and informed consent, these forms are provided for informational purposes only, and are not intended to substitute for the judgment of an attorney licensed to practice in your state.

Statutes That Might Affect You

Most states have laws against practicing medicine without a license, but what is meant by "practicing medicine?" Every state defines this phrase differently, either through statute or case law. Penalties can be severe. (In Illinois, for example, the unauthorized practice of medicine is a felony. Unauthorized practice of medicine includes not only diagnosing and treating illnesses, but also attaching the title "Doctor" to your name to represent yourself as authorized to treat illnesses.) Clearly, no personal trainer should attempt to treat diseases or other medical problems, either with supplements, special diets, or similar modalities.

Your clients might ask your advice on the treatment of injuries. You should always preface any response to questions about treating injuries with the statement, "Of course, I'm not a doctor, and I can't diagnose your injury," or something similar. Limit your advice to general statements about RICE (Rest, Ice, Compression, and Elevation) and recommend that your clients see their physicians for diagnosis and treatment of injuries. Continue to monitor reported injuries by asking your client to keep a written diary about them and report on their progress regularly so that you can make necessary modifications in their workouts.

Some states regulate activities that personal trainers sometimes engage in. For example, in Illinois, there is a statute that regulates the giving of advice on nutrition. Your state may have similar laws or regulations. Consult with a licensed attorney to find out what restrictions affect you.

CHAPTER 3

Marketing Your Business

Marketing is simply promoting your business and attracting clients. You should approach marketing your business just as you approach any important project, by setting objectives and mapping out the steps to reach them. Think of it this way: Somewhere out there are scads of people who will benefit from working with you. They're just waiting for you to reach out, tap them on the shoulder, and tell them how you can enrich their lives. That's where marketing comes in.

Who Is Your Customer?

Identifying your target market—answering the questions "Who do I want to work with?" and "How do I reach them?"—is your first step in getting clients. You might be thinking, "I'll work with anyone! I just want to do personal training!" What's wrong with that? Simply this: You can't do everything and do everything well. Remember, your goal is to be the best in your field, and to be your best, you need to concentrate on what you do best. You shouldn't decide that you want to train bodybuilders preparing for competition if your background is primarily in teaching aerobics. If you spent several years in competitive swimming, you'd be uniquely qualified to work with swimmers, designing programs to help them improve their performance. A woman in my master's program, a student who returned to school after raising her family, decided that she wants to work with physically active people over age 50 who live or work near her home. This is her target market. Here are a few exercises to help you get started finding yours.

List Your Special Qualifications

Write a list of your unique qualifications. What benefits can you offer people that someone else with similar education cannot? Have you participated in a sport in addition to weight training? For example, are you a golfer, tennis player, or swimmer who can coach these sports as well as provide advice on general conditioning?

Write a Profile of Your Ideal Customer

Be as specific as possible. How old is she? Where does she live? What sports does she do? What does she do for a living? What is her annual income? It's important to get a clear picture of this client, so spend some time and effort doing it. After you have come up with a specific, detailed picture of your customer, you will be able to find her.

Envision Reaching Your Customer

You wouldn't reach middle-aged executives who like to play golf by advertising in a decorating magazine, would you? Of course not. Since you've clearly defined your customer, you shouldn't have any problem figuring out where he likes to go and what he likes to do.

1. Where does your ideal customer go on a regular basis?

2. What publications does your ideal customer read?

3. In what activities does your ideal customer like to participate?

Outline a Strategy

With this information in hand, start planning your marketing strategy. For example, after doing a little snooping around, you determine that most of the people in your target market shop regularly at a small sporting goods store downtown. You also learn that most of the people in your target market read the afternoon paper. You should approach the store's owners about putting some of your business cards by the register, and place an attractive display ad in the afternoon paper. Then wait for your phone to ring!

Advertising

Many personal trainers have begun their businesses with one well-designed, well-placed ad. Once you have identified your target market, you should be able to figure out where and when to run this special ad and what it should say.

Sometimes newspapers or magazines offer small businesses substantially discounted rates if they agree to advertise every week, or at some other regular interval for an extended period of time. While this seems like a bargain, it will be one only if the ad pulls in customers. Otherwise, it will be a millstone around your neck, taking dollars away from what would otherwise be an effective marketing program. Try a single ad in the paper and see how that works for you. If you get enough calls, consider asking the ad representative about discounted rates.

Referrals

Some of the best methods won't cost you anything! Without a doubt, word of mouth is the very best source of new clients. The fact that your current client recommends you sells you as a competent, professional personal trainer. Being recommended by a client is one of the highest forms of praise you can get!

Referrals from other professionals also cost you nothing. One advantage of getting at least a bachelor's degree in exercise physiology, exercise science, or a related field is that you will have a much easier time marketing your services to physicians, chiropractors, physical therapists, and other health professionals. It's not that only people with degrees know anything. I know some competent, excellent personal trainers who are self-educated. It might seem unfair, but health professionals, wary of liability and degreed themselves, tend to be extremely reluctant to recommend anyone without formal credentials. If you have a degree and are certified by a reputable organization, you can confidently approach health professionals and offer your services to help them get their patients started on safe, effective fitness programs.

Marketing Materials

Sometimes people ask me how to come up with a business name. Everyone wants something clever, but not cutesy, something everyone will remember. Unfortunately, there's no easy way to find these little gems. In my experience, the best ones are often the result of serendipity. They seem to sprout from that special precious spot in the brain, pass through the heart, and spring to our consciousness. ("A-ha!") Failing an "a-ha," you could do some brainstorming, either alone or with friends. Write down without hesitation everything that occurs to you and see if anything inspired pops out. If not, don't despair. There's nothing wrong with using your name, and there's at least one advantage: You don't have to do any costly name searches to see if anyone is already using your perfect name.

Your Business Card

The most important marketing piece you have is your business card (see figure 3.1). It is the item that most people will keep and remember you by, so get the best quality card you can. Do everything possible to make it look professional. Use high quality paper. Strongly consider hiring a graphic designer to come up with a logo for your company.

A word about titles: If you don't have a master's degree, should you put any initials after your name? I suggest simply the title "Personal Trainer" under your name. Sometime when I wasn't looking, some trainers started using the initials "CPT," which I now realize mean "Certified Personal Trainer," after their names. I've seen this title a lot lately, especially in health clubs. (The first time I saw this CPT business, I thought the card's presenter was a physical therapist!) Perhaps it's my legal background, but I'm not sure I can recommend that approach. It seems like a misrepresentation. It always appears to me that the

Positive Image

Consultation & Fitness Training

Your name
Personal Trainer

708•555•1212

Figure 3.1   Sample business card.

person is trying to overstate his credentials, as if he's saying, "No, I don't have a degree, so I can't use the initials MS, MD, or PhD, so I'll use some other initials. Maybe if I'm lucky they'll get confused and think I'm a physical therapist or something." Most people are not fooled by this, at least not those who can afford to pay your fee, and it only calls attention to the fact that you don't have a master's degree. List your phone number and a catchy tag line if you've been able to think of one.

Brochures and Leaflets

A business card is really the only essential marketing piece that you need. If you desire, and if you have invested the time and effort in creating a logo, have some brochures printed to help promote your business. Describe the benefits of your service and any special features you offer. Not only do you not have to, I suggest you don't, spend an arm and a leg on these. I'm not saying you should create some cheesy looking thing that could be mistaken for a ransom note, but it's the content that counts most. As with your business card, use quality paper and spend some time considering the design of the piece, but remember that the most important aspect of the brochure is substance, not style. Give serious thought to what makes you special and sets your service apart and the best way to present it.

Your First Contact

The first time you talk to your prospective new client, you will have a limited amount of time to impress her with your professionalism, knowledge, and infectious enthusiasm. Typically, your first contact will be over the phone. Begin by asking how she heard about you. This information sets the tone for the rest of the conversation. If she heard about you from one of your current customers, you don't have to spend as much time giving her your entire educational and professional biography, although you should still give basic information. If she is responding to an ad, encourage her to tell you about her current fitness situation and what she hopes you can do for her.

What comes next depends on how serious you perceive this prospect to be. Let's face it: You'd like to work with everyone, but there is only one of you and you have to ration your precious time carefully, if not ruthlessly. Everyone wants to know how much things cost, of course, but if a prospect seems concerned about cost to the exclusion of everything else, I suggest that you send her a rate card describing your services and the prices for each. If price, not quality, is a prospect's primary concern, why spend a lot of time describing all of your qualifications? If you are a well-educated professional, you will never be able to compete on price, since, as we have discussed, the world is full of less-than-qualified people who are willing to work for slightly above minimum wage. Let your rate card speak for you. On the other hand, if after a few minutes of conversation it is apparent that this prospect really wants to work with you, and she hasn't asked you yet about price, you should tell her your rates. If she isn't scared off by that, arrange a meeting at a mutually convenient time and place.

This meeting is for both you and your potential client. I strongly believe that before either of you enter into any sort of trainer-client relationship, you should meet, talk briefly, and make sure you're comfortable with each other. If you're planning to work out in the client's home, meet there. That will give you the opportunity to inventory the available equipment, see the available space, and otherwise prepare for any special needs dictated by the workout area. If you'll be working out in a club or gym, the meeting gives the client a chance to see the facility, find out about memberships, and get comfortable there. Bring your packet of new client forms with you to this meeting. If all goes well, congratulations—you have a client!

What to Do Before Meeting With Your First Prospective Client

- Do you have current knowledge of anatomy, physiology, and biomechanics? In short, do you know what you're doing?

- Are you certified by a reputable organization?

- Do you have liability insurance?

- Do you have the following forms?
  - Health history questionnaire
  - Waivers
  - Goal inventory

- Has your waiver form been reviewed by an attorney licensed to practice in your state?

- Do you have written policies in place regarding payment, cancellation, and credits for cancelled workouts?

- Do you have current CPR certification?

- Do you have a separate business checking account?

- Do you have a bookkeeping system in place?

- Do you have all required business licenses and/or other permits required by your city or state?

- Do you have a separate phone line for your business, or at least have you made arrangements to have your business calls handled professionally?

Things to Make Sure Your New Client Has, on or Before Your First Meeting

- Brochure
- Business card
- Letter of agreement
- Waivers
- Health history questionnaire
- Goal inventory
- Self-addressed, stamped envelope (if you plan on having the forms mailed back to you)

Keeping Track of the Results

After you've been at this for a while, you will discover what methods of reaching potential customers are most successful. Of course, the sooner you obtain this information, the less time and money you'll waste building your client base. You could spend months sitting around twiddling your thumbs because you select the wrong advertising vehicle, only to switch and find yourself working nonstop. At this point, you'll be thinking, "Where were you (successful ad vehicle) several hundred (or, God forbid, thousand) dollars ago?" You can avoid asking this question by asking prospects who call how they heard about you. Chart this information and cut your losses.

PART II

WORKING
WITH
YOUR CLIENT

CHAPTER 4

Creating Your Client's Program

Your client hired you for a number of reasons. He might want someone to provide motivation and encourage him as he reaches his fitness goals and makes the sometimes tricky transition from food junkie to healthful eater. He might want to have a regular appointment to force him to be consistent with exercise. In many cases, though, the number-one reason clients hire us is to have someone show them what to do and how to do it correctly. You probably know that a lot of confusion exists about which exercises to do for what. When you throw in the variables of age, medical history, and previous injuries, many people will simply throw up their hands and decide they'd be better off just sitting on the couch. That's where you come in.

General Principles of Program Design

The first step in designing your client's program is gathering information, through both your fitness assessment and health history questionnaires. We'll discuss those topics in detail in chapter 5, but first let's review some general principles that apply to every client's program.

- A well-designed fitness program is complete.
- A well-designed fitness program has four components:
  1. Resistance training
  2. Cardiovascular conditioning
  3. Flexibility training
  4. Proper nutrition
- A program that does not include all four components is incomplete and will not accomplish the goal of a strong, healthy body.

Factors to Consider When Designing Your Client's Program

- Age
- Previous training
- Previous injuries
- Health history
- Medical restrictions
- Current physical condition
- Time available per week
- Time available per session
- Equipment available
- Client's desires
- Client's goals and objectives
- Client's life situation
- Client's personality

- A well-designed fitness program reflects an understanding of human movement and basic principles of biomechanics. A safe, effective strength and conditioning program depends on developing balance between the joints on both sides of the body.

- A well-designed fitness program is based on clearly defined, appropriate goals and objectives.

- A well-designed fitness program results from carefully creating and planning appropriate individualized goals and objectives. When I talk to groups, I am often asked, "What should I do to get in shape?" This is a lot like someone asking, "How do I get there?" without telling you where "there" is. You can't design an effective program for a person without understanding her specific goals and objectives.

- A well-designed fitness program is customized. No two people are exactly the same. Your exercise prescription must reflect this fact. One-size-fits-all programs don't fit anyone properly.

What's the Point?

You should ask, "What is the objective?" about every exercise. The term *objective* in this book has a dual meaning. First, it is the rationale for everything in your client's program. Why do you want your client to do leg extensions? Why are you using a free weight exercise rather than a machine to work a particular muscle group? Your objectives will provide sound answers to these questions. Second, the objective is the guide and goal for your client. Once you've decided to include a particular exercise in the routine, explain what you want your client to do. In the case of leg extensions, you'll see much better form if you say, "Your objective is to straighten your legs at the knee joints while keeping your hips relaxed."

Objectives of a Good Wellness Program
• Condition all major muscle groups
• Increase and maintain flexibility
• Avoid injury
• Maintain consistency
• Develop a strong sense of self-efficacy
• Develop body awareness
• Achieve and maintain functional posture
• Incorporate healthful nutrition and activity habits into the client's lifestyle
• Improve or maintain health

The Resistance Component

It is no longer in doubt: Everyone should do some form of resistance training, to prevent injury, to increase metabolism, to improve sports performance, and to maintain function as we get older. Resistance training, also known as strength training, is deliberate activity designed to strengthen and condition muscle tissue using equipment such as weights, machines, or elastic tubing. Of course, like all the other components of your client's program, the resistance portion requires that you give some thought to his specific needs and objectives. More on that in a minute. First, let's review some basic biomechanical concepts.

Everything You Ever Needed to Know About Resistance Training You Learned in Sixth-Grade Science

Understanding human movement is critical to designing effective programs and instructing your clients about how to do their workouts correctly. Remember that the body is a system of pulleys and levers. When you use a wrench to loosen a nut from a bolt, you exert a force against the lever (the wrench), which is connected to a fixed pivot point. Similarly, during movement, the bones (levers) move around fixed pivot points, the joints, when a force is exerted against the lever by muscle. Why is this important to understand? First, understanding the axis of rotation and the lever being moved directs your attention to the targeted muscle or muscle group. Second, once you focus your client's attention on the targeted muscle, you can keep your eagle eye on making sure he's not using other muscles or committing other form flaws that reduce the effectiveness of the exercise.

What Is the Pivot Point?

The pivot point is the axis of rotation, the joint that the bone rotates around (see figure 4.1). This is not simply a matter of academic interest, it has major practical implications for your client's form on every exercise. In a barbell curl, for example, the pivot point is the elbow. Since this is a single-joint movement, the shoulder joint is not also a pivot point. The practical implication is that the upper arms must stay stationary against the body throughout the range of motion.

Where Is the Center of Gravity?

On some exercises, it's critical that the client have her weight distributed in a particular fashion. For example, when instructing a client on doing a squat, you should explain the importance of shifting weight onto the heels to make sure she drops her glutes and flexes at the hip, thereby taking stress off the knees. On some other exercises, such as lunges, it's important to keep the center of gravity in the power core (low back and abdominals) for balance.

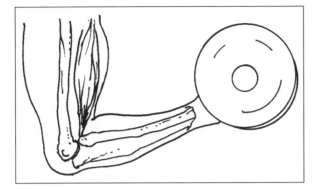

Figure 4.1   The pivot point.

Which Muscles Are the Prime Movers?

You need to know which muscles are prime movers so you can focus your client's attention on the targeted muscle or muscle group and help him make the mind-muscle connection that makes the exercise more effective. This information can make each repetition a focused, effective effort instead of a ballistic, flopping waste of time.

What Is the Plane of Motion?

Since the body is three-dimensional, anatomists divide the body into fixed reference points called body planes to describe its structure. Taking a cue from them, I use the phrase "plane of motion" to explain the proper position of body segments during specific exercises. As you can see in figure 4.2, visualizing these "slices" through the body allows you to understand, and to explain to your client, the relationship of different body segments to one another during exercises. This is important because your client needs to remember to keep the moving body part in the proper alignment so that the targeted muscle will do the work. For example, if he is doing a dumbbell shoulder press, he needs to keep his arms in the same plane as his head to avoid the tendency to move them forward into an inclined position where pectorals, rather than the targeted deltoids, do most of the work.

What Is the Relationship of the Involved Joints to Each Other?

In some exercises, it is important to keep the joints in the proper position to work the targeted muscle in its own distinctive line of pull. For example, beginners might have a difficult time understanding that it is possible to move the upper arms without also

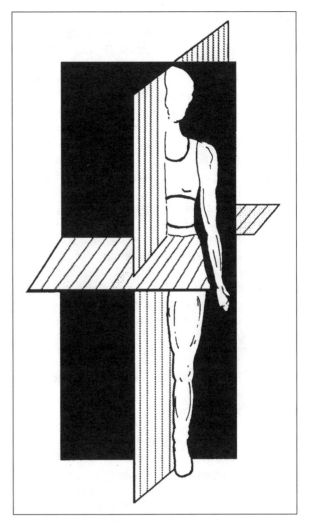

Figure 4.2   The plane of motion.

elevating the scapula. By educating your client about the distinct nature of these two structures, you can dramatically improve her form on multijoint upper-body movements. Keeping these relationships correct can also prevent injury to your client. For example, in the squat, your client should flex not only at the knees, but also at the hips to avoid excessive knee flexion.

Is This a Single- or Multijoint Movement?

We use the terms *single-joint* and *multijoint* to refer to the primary axis (or axes) of rotation and to help the client visualize how to perform movements with proper form. Some single-joint movements actually involve more than one joint, but not as a primary axis. For example, we refer to the dumbbell fly as a single-joint movement. During this exercise, the primary axis of rotation is the shoulder, so you should emphasize to your client that he should not flex and extend at the elbow. Single-joint movements are rotary (curved) movements, while multijoint movements are linear (straight). Single-joint movements are most effective in isolating a particular muscle, while multijoint movements involve several muscles.

This information is vital to your program design. Awareness of single-joint and multijoint movements will help you teach (and clients practice) correct form. Clients who understand that a triceps pushdown is a single-joint movement also understand that they must keep their upper arms stationary to avoid shoulder flexion. In general, it's best to do a multijoint movement before a single-joint movement involving one of the active muscle groups. For example, a client should do a dumbbell bench press first, working pectorals, anterior deltoids, and triceps, and then do dumbbell flys to isolate the pectorals. (This assumes you aren't working with an advanced client who wants to pre-exhaust the pectorals first.)

Is This Exercise Safe for This Client?

As you know, certain exercises have earned the designation *contraindicated*. This means that experts have determined that the risk of injury from doing them outweighs the potential benefit for most people. There are other exercises that, while safe for most healthy individuals, might be contraindicated for your client because of her unique physical condition. Your initial evaluation will determine which exercises to eliminate or modify to protect your client from injury.

Free Weights or Machines?

Frequently you will be asked whether it's better for someone to train with weights or machines. As you've probably guessed, there is no right answer. Each type of equipment has advantages and disadvantages for each individual. The short answer is that in general, most people need to use free weights at least some of the time to gain functional strength, that is, the type of strength we use in daily activities. Think about it: When you have to carry a bag of groceries, you use not only the directly involved muscles, but also the deep muscles that stabilize your limbs and joints. When you lift a free weight, these stabilizers have to do some work. When you use a machine, it does the stabilizing; you just have to push, pull, or curl using the muscles targeted by the exercise. Free weight movements are generally

more challenging and more advanced. Consequently, some unconditioned clients might need to begin on machines with certain movements until they develop a good base of strength to prepare them for the challenge of free weights.

Clients who are rehabilitating from injuries might need to limit their work on certain muscle groups or joints to machines until they are pain free. With sedentary beginners, especially those over 40, I usually begin with machines (if available) on the multijoint exercises for large muscle groups—for example, the bench press. After three or four weeks, I introduce the free weight version of the exercise using very light resistance. But this is not a hard and fast rule that you should apply to all of your clients. As in every other aspect of your duties as a professional, you must use your knowledge and judgment.

How Much Weight Should I Use?

Selecting the appropriate weight is both an art and a science—it requires the creativity and flexibility of an artist as well as the precision and sound judgment of a scientist. During your initial assessment of your client, you will do a series of strength tests that will give you some information to guide you in selecting appropriate weights. Table 4.1 shows general guidelines for selecting beginning weights based on percentage of body weight. The following suggestions will also help.

Keep in mind that while a given amount of weight—say 30 pounds—is always the same, it might not always require the same amount of force to move. The number of pulleys, the design of a particular machine, and the quality of maintenance will affect how hard it is to perform one rep. Don't assume that your client should use the same weight at every club or machine.

The first few times performing a new motor activity are often awkward, jerky, and uncomfortable. Lifting weights is no exception, so initially select a weight that is about 25 percent less than you think will be manageable for your client.

I don't believe in giving one-repetition maximum (often called one-rep max) tests to beginners, and it should be obvious why. Beginners do not have the experience and body awareness to lift heavy resistance safely. You can approximate a one-rep max test by selecting a resistance that you think your client can lift eight times. The last two reps should be challenging enough that you might have to give your client a little spot. Multiply the resistance by 1.27 to get an approximation of your client's one-rep max. A beginning client should be able to lift a

Table 4.1 General Guidelines for Selecting Beginning Weights

		Upper body		Lower body	
Male		**Warm-up**	**First set**	**Warm-up**	**First set**
Free weight	(SJ)	15-20%	25-30%	30-50%	50-70%
Free weight	(MJ)	10-20%	30-40%	50-70%	100-120%
Machine	(SJ)	15-20%	25-30%	20-30%	30-60%
Machine	(MJ)	20-25%	30-50%	50-60%	100-150%
Female		**Warm-up**	**First set**	**Warm-up**	**First set**
Free weight	(SJ)	5-10%	10-12%	20-30%	40-50%
Free weight	(MJ)	15-20%	20-30%	40-50%	70-100%
Machine	(SJ)	10-15%	15-25%	15-20%	30-50%
Machine	(MJ)	20-25%	25-40%	40-50%	80-100%

Note: Percentages refer to percentage of body weight. These percentages are only guidelines for selecting appropriate resistance, based on my work with a diverse client base. Every client has individual needs. Be sure to consider principles of good program design and the objectives of the client's program when selecting appropriate weights. Adjust the resistance after the warm-up to make sure the client can perform 8 to 12 repetitions (upper body) or 12 to 15 repetitions (lower body) with good form.

SJ = single-joint
MJ = multijoint

resistance at least 12 times under control with the last two or three reps being challenging. Generally, this will be 75 percent of the one-rep max. Remember, though, this is only a guideline.

Beginners should never lift heavy weights, defined as a resistance so heavy that the client cannot control it alone, or do at least 10 repetitions without the help of a spotter. Lifting excessive resistance, especially in the beginning stages of a program, can result in tendinitis or other injury. Recall also that you need to take the client's whole body and its condition into account, not just the muscles and joints involved in the exercise.

Consider the squat, for example. I often share this gym mantra with my clients: "The squat is the king of exercises." The squat earned this lofty title by effectively working so many muscles with one movement. This efficiency doesn't come without a price, though. The weightlifter performing the squat must be conditioned not only in his hamstrings and quadriceps, but also in his abdominals and low back. He must also have sufficient flexibility in his shoulder (rotator cuff, specifically) to hold a bar behind his neck and enough arm and shoulder strength to keep the bar from rolling down his back. Your new client's quadriceps and hamstrings may indeed be strong enough to flex and extend his knee, espe-

cially with a very lightweight bar, but are his abdominals and low back strong enough to support his spine in the proper alignment and to allow him to do the exercise with correct form? Is his rotator cuff flexible enough to allow him to hold his shoulders in abduction and external rotation for the time needed to do the exercise? You get the idea. Don't think of your client as a collection of muscles and joints, each with a given ability to generate force. Consider the whole human being!

Troubleshooting

There are a number of problems you could run into, as I'll describe in the following section. But remember that not all will apply to every client.

Discrepancies in Muscle Size

Every multijoint exercise is a team effort, but not every member of the team is the same size. One

Always err on the light side. You can always make the weight heavier, but the time to find out it's too heavy isn't after your client is lying in a heap on the floor!

muscle or muscle group is smaller than all the others, and must use a greater percentage of its force-generating ability to move the resistance than a larger muscle will. For example, if you do a lat pulldown with 100 pounds, you are using your latissimus dorsi, rhomboids, posterior deltoids, biceps, and forearms. Your back looks at this 100 pounds and says, "That looks like a good, challenging resistance to move," but your forearms say, "You want me to move what?!"

Discrepancies in the Rate That Body Structures Strengthen

You need to consider not just muscles, but also tendons and ligaments when you select exercises and weight amounts. I cannot emphasize enough the importance of remembering that muscles get stronger much quicker than tendons and ligaments! Tendons and ligaments transmit the force generated by the muscles to complete movement and maintain the integrity of joints. They will get stronger, just as muscles will, but take more time. Excessive amounts of weight, especially used by beginners and older, poorly conditioned clients can result in severe tendinitis.

Conditioning in the Power Core

Sometimes trainers exhibit the unfortunate shortsightedness that has often plagued businesses and governments. As in the case of these institutions, the results can be disastrous. Specifically, these trainers focus on developing specific muscles or muscle groups and neglect the important need to strengthen the power core, or the abdominals and low back (see figure 4.3). Resist the tendency to emphasize the Hollywood muscles—the biceps, triceps, chest, and deltoids—to the exclusion of these vital trunk muscles. Beginners especially need to develop strength and flexibility in the abdominals and low back. If you include plenty of basic multijoint movements in your client's program, the smaller, show-off muscles will reach a level of basic conditioning that will prepare them for the more specific, intense workouts to come. The patience and long-range thinking reflected by your intelligent program design will be rewarded when your client's strong power core provides a stable base for arm and shoulder movements.

Considerations Unique to a Particular Client

A particular client might have a condition that creates a problem with training. Continuing with the lat pulldown example, suppose your client is a golfer

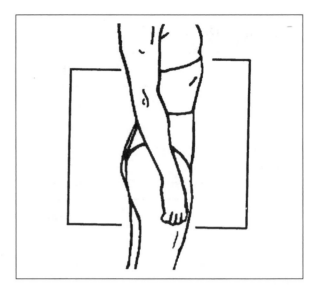

Figure 4.3   The power core.

who has suffered chronic elbow tendinitis. Wrist flexion and extension will aggravate this condition, as will gripping. Therefore, even though he might be able to move a heavier weight, you should err on the side of what the forearms can handle. (This rule might dictate your eliminating the exercise altogether.) Another example is a very poorly conditioned beginner who may have a difficult time doing a lat pulldown because of weakness in the low back and abdominals. She might not have the strength to hold her body at a 45 degree angle while doing the exercise. Her condition will dictate that you begin by strengthening the low back and abdominals and use a different exercise such as a dumbbell row or seated row to work the latissimus dorsi and rhomboids.

Keep in mind that some exercises are generally contraindicated and should not be performed in any circumstance. Some of these exercises are illustrated in figures 4.4 to 4.17.

Ensuring Correct Form

For every exercise, it is important that you understand and are able to explain to your client all of the following:

- Pivot point or points (the joint or joints that are the axis or axes of rotation)
- Lever (the bone or bones being moved)
- Plane of motion (frontal, sagittal, horizontal)
- Puller or pusher (the muscle or muscles providing the force for the movement)
- Position (the relationship of the joints to each other)

Figure 4.4   Unsupported spinal flexion, especially with twisting.

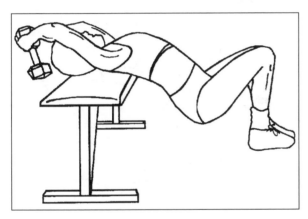

Figure 4.5   Pullovers across a bench.

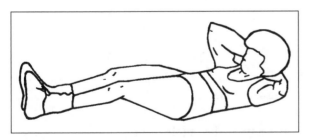

Figure 4.6   Straight leg sit-ups.

If you do understand and explain these points to your client, you will be able to correct form mistakes and make the workout more effective. I periodically give my clients little pop quizzes prior to certain exercises just to help them learn and understand these critical elements for every exercise. I might say, "Mary, can you describe the relationship be-

Figure 4.7   Hurdler stretch.

Figure 4.8   Deep squats (more than 90 degrees of knee flexion).

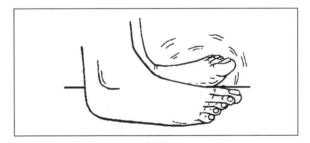

Figure 4.9   Barefoot exercise.

tween the shoulders and elbows in this movement?" or, "What is the axis of rotation in this exercise?" You need to constantly reinforce your client's knowledge.

Increasing Difficulty

In order for exercise to continue to help your client make progress toward her goals, it must be progressive; that is, it must continue to challenge her muscles to get stronger by imposing greater demands on them. In the beginning, nearly every exercise will be

Figure 4.10   Ballistic stretches.

Figure 4.11   Bouncing hyperextension of back.

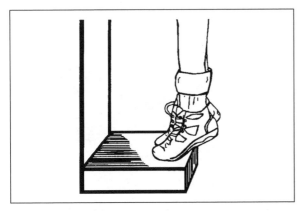

Figure 4.12   Ankle weights.

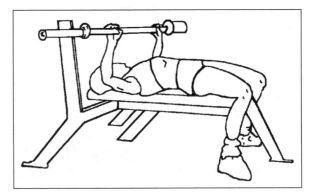

Figure 4.13   Bridging (arching the back during a bench press).

Figure 4.14   Lifting leg above body when on all fours.

Figure 4.15   Fire hydrants.

challenging, but after a few weeks or months (everyone is different), you will need to ratchet the intensity upward to keep things moving in the right direction.

There are four ways to increase the difficulty of an exercise:

1. Increase the amount of resistance
2. Shorten the amount of rest between sets
3. Increase the number of repetitions
4. Change exercise order

Heavier Is not Necessarily Better

The most obvious (but not always the best) way to increase the intensity of an exercise is to increase the amount of resistance. Do so cautiously. Remember that it takes longer for tendons to adjust to the

Figure 4.16   Plow.

Figure 4.17   Ballistic movements.

demands of heavier resistance. If you increase the amount of weight too dramatically, your client might develop a nasty case of chronic tendinitis that will retard her progress for months. To avoid this risk, begin with a weight that your client can lift with good form for 12 repetitions. The last two or three repetitions should be challenging. When this weight is no longer challenging, increase weight no more than five percent and have your client perform eight repetitions. When this weight is challenging, increase another five percent, and so on.

Time Is the Tyrant

It amazes me to see trainers not monitoring the rest intervals that their clients take between sets. Decreasing the rest period from one minute, which is fairly typical, to 40 seconds will increase intensity dramatically. Try it yourself—you'll be amazed. (The one certain exception to this rule is abdominals,

where you should keep the rest short, just 10-20 seconds. The key to effective abdominals training is working them very intensely for a short time.) I use a watch with a timer to keep track of rest intervals. It's important to have a system for keeping track of time, since during the rest interval you and your client will be reviewing form points, or just generally gabbing away. I've found that decreasing the rest interval is a very effective way to increase intensity without some of the risks inherent in increasing the amount of resistance. Consider using this method with smaller muscle groups such as arms, where tendinitis is always a possibility.

A Numbers Game

The optimal number of repetitions depends on the desired objective. If you're trying to develop pure strength, generally you will want to use heavier resistance and fewer repetitions; however, this protocol is appropriate only for advanced weight trainers. Beginners should train in the 8 to 12 repetition range, since this is the optimal number for increasing strength and endurance and improving overall conditioning. Increasing the number of repetitions is a safe, effective way to increase training effort and strength stimulus.

Changing Exercise Order

A typical workout routine is designed to work muscles from large to small; that is, legs, back, chest, shoulders, triceps, biceps, and forearms, doing multijoint exercises first, then single-joint isolation movements. (Abdominals can be done before or after the routine.) While this order has its advantages, namely that the biggest muscles are worked in the beginning when energy levels should be highest, it has one notable disadvantage. The large muscles are best worked by basic multijoint exercises, which involve not only the prime mover, but also smaller helper muscles. For example, the targeted muscle in the bench press is the pectorals, but it's impossible to perform the exercise without a lot of other role players: deltoids, triceps, and the rotator cuff. When confronted with resistance, these smaller muscles fatigue much sooner than the larger pectorals. Once the triceps are done, your client is done bench pressing. But the pectorals are thinking, "Whew, that was easy. Dodged a bullet there. I could do at least four more repetitions." What if instead you had your client perform an isolation exercise for pectorals first, and then do the bench press? The triceps and shoulders would still be fresh, but the pectorals would go into the bench press like an NBA team on a 12-day road trip, pre-exhausted. That is, in fact, what this technique is called—pre-exhaustion. It's a terrific way to increase intensity, but it should be used only with advanced trainees, not beginners.

Pace of Repetitions

You've probably seen someone in the gym writhing and contorting, practically doing a backbend, while a blur of something passes in front of him. After a few seconds, you realize that the blur is actually a barbell that he is hurling up and down with the momentum of his undulating spine. Effective? Yes, if the objective is to see how much weight he can move without regard to which muscles do the moving or to the potential for injury. The more momentum used to move a resistance, the greater the risk of injury, the greater trauma to joints and surrounding structures, and the less work performed by the targeted muscle. To avoid this sort of thing, I suggest to my clients that they maintain a slow, steady pace, especially on the negative portion of the exercise.

One exception to this rule: If you are coaching your client with a view to improving her performance in a sport in which speed matters, you need to add some fast-paced training to her regime. This type of training is safe and effective if done with extremely low resistance (body weight segments, a golf club, a medicine ball) under control.

Range of Motion (ROM)

In general, you should instruct your client to move the resistance through a full range of motion. There might be situations in which you will find it desirable to limit the range of motion of a particular exercise. For example, if your client has been experiencing some shoulder tendinitis, he should limit his range of motion on the flat dumbbell press by refraining from lowering his upper arms below the plane of the bench, at least until he is pain free and has medical clearance to resume full ROM.

You'll be able to tell when your client is reaching momentary muscular failure when he starts voluntarily (he might even say it was involuntary—"I swear I couldn't help it!") limiting his ROM. Encourage him to maintain his perfect form despite fatigue and muscle-searing lactic acid. When he can't do so any longer, the set is over.

Vary the Routine

Some chronic injuries that bedevil weight trainers, especially those over 30, are the result of repetitive motion. For example, tendinitis and more serious conditions can result from performing the same movements constantly, especially with heavy weights. You increase this risk dramatically by not conditioning both sides of a joint, thereby creating dangerous strength imbalances. Some suggestions for avoiding this potential problem follow.

Change Your Client's Routine Periodically

Vary aspects of your client's routine. Beginners' routines should change every six to eight weeks. More advanced clients can benefit from short (two- to four-week) phases focusing on particular muscle groups, or on achieving gains in strength or power.

Rotate Exercises Within Phases

Design your routines so that the client does different exercises for all major muscle groups. Unless she is preparing for a bench press contest, for example, no client should bench press every time she works out. This is asking for a shoulder problem. Plan a workout that is all single-joint isolation movements or one that gives your client a break from weights and uses different types of resistance (medicine balls, bands). In my experience, this sort of variety not only helps avoid injury, it keeps workouts interesting and fun, and thereby beats two motivation killers, boredom and burnout.

Pay Close Attention to Aches and Pains

Often chronic injuries begin insidiously. A slight twinge on shoulder abduction after performing a set of machine shoulder presses can be the beginning of a serious injury. Take these things seriously. If a client tells you over and over again about a persistent ache or pain, especially when doing a particular exercise, redesign your routine to avoid stressing the area. If rest doesn't result in significant improvement within two weeks, strongly recommend that your client consult a physician. Never attempt to diagnose injuries on your own! What might seem like tendinitis to you could be some underlying pathology that will benefit from immediate medical intervention.

Failure Can Be Good

I always tell my clients that the gym is the only place where failure is the result you actually hope for, and that it's OK, even desirable, to have negative thoughts. By that I mean that we want to work to the point of momentary muscular failure on the last rep or two; that is, take the muscle to the point of complete fatigue so it will come back stronger.

Normally, I think negative thoughts are nothing short of poison to the spirit and the mind, but I actually encourage my clients to think negatively when it comes to weight training. I want them to use the negative: Lowering the resistance slowly, resisting the effects of gravity while the muscle is lengthening, makes the muscle produce much more force and dramatically improves the effectiveness of resistance training. I suggest that you have your client perform the positive part of the movement to a count of two and the negative to a count of four.

> Failure is a good thing. It's not only OK to be negative—I encourage it.

The Cardiovascular Component

Most people know that they need to do cardiovascular (CV) exercise in addition to resistance training. In fact, the understanding that "exercise" means something other than just CV exercise is a relatively recent development. What is cardiovascular exercise?

Cardiovascular exercise improves the ability of the lungs to provide oxygen and the heart and vessels to supply blood to the tissues. CV exercise achieves these improvements by working large muscles in a continuous, rhythmic fashion for a prolonged period of time. Examples include, but are certainly not limited to, walking, jogging, running, in-line skating, cycling, stairstepping, rowing, and cross-country skiing.

Planning for Progress

ACSM has identified three stages of progression in cardiovascular fitness programs:

1. Initial conditioning
2. Improvement conditioning
3. Maintenance

In the initial conditioning stage, which usually lasts four to six weeks, the client should do low level aerobic exercise every other day for 10 to 15 minutes. It's important during this stage to err on the low side of intensity to allow your client to adapt to the new demands exercise places on his body and prepare him for the improvement stage. During the improvement stage (four to five months), you can begin to increase both the intensity and duration of your client's cardiovascular sessions.

Depending on how well your client adapts to increased demands, you can increase the duration of

---

> **ACSM Guidelines for Designing CV Exercise**
>
> - **Frequency of exercise.** Three to five days per week
> - **Intensity of exercise.** Physical activity corresponding to 40 to 85 percent of $\dot{V}O_2$max or 60 to 90 percent of maximal heart rate
> - **Duration of exercise.** Fifteen to 60 minutes of continuous or discontinuous aerobic activity per session

each CV session by up to several minutes every two to three weeks. If he handles increased time with minimal difficulty, gradually increase intensity, too, so that at the end of this stage your client has reached a targeted level of intensity (usually 60 to 90 percent of maximal heart rate) and is able to maintain this pace for a minimum of 20 minutes. During maintenance (six months after beginning and beyond), most clients will be satisfied with their level of cardiovascular conditioning, but might occasionally need a tune-up, or a review and re-assessment of their goals and objectives. Perhaps you might introduce new methods and types of exercise to eliminate the risk of boredom and dropping out. All of your clients' programs should include CV exercise, but each client's CV exercise, just like resistance training, must be designed especially for him. Following are the principles that should guide your design.

Frequency

I aim for a minimum of three sessions per week, and suggest as many as five for clients seriously intent on losing large amounts of body fat in a minimal period of time. Occasionally, clients want to know if it's OK to do CV exercise every day. The answer is usually yes, with an explanation. The explanation is that while it is perfectly all right to do some type of CV exercise every day, it's not advisable to do a high-intensity, long CV session every day. Such zealotry can lead to overtraining, injury, and illness. (For many clients, wondering if it's all right to do CV every day will be the least of their problems. Finding time to do it even three days a week can be a challenge for many clients, what with careers, travel, and family demands.)

Intensity

Since most of you don't have access to a lab where you can do a $\dot{V}O_2$max test, you will have to employ more primitive, but no less effective means to get the information you need. Use a test that you're familiar and comfortable with to establish your client's baseline level of cardiovascular fitness and to decide where to begin and what your short-term and intermediate goals are. Your client's current resting heart rate (RHR) is a good indication of cardiovascular fitness.

You'll also need to compute your client's target heart rate (THR) and maximum heart rate (MHR). Most of you are familiar with the formula

THR = Heart Rate Reserve x Desired Intensity + RHR.

In this equation, heart rate reserve is the difference between maximum heart rate and resting heart rate. The desired intensity referred to is the percentage of maximum heart rate that you select given your client's current condition and desired objectives (that 60-90 percent of maximum heart rate referred to above). Isolating your client's specific resting heart rate and then adding it back provides a more accurate, customized result than simply taking a percentage of MHR.

Recently, there has been concern that the predicted MHR of 220 minus the client's age is less than an absolute formula. Aerobics pioneer Ken Cooper suggests that for fit males, 205 minus .5 times age is a more accurate way to calculate MHR. Some have suggested that for women, who have smaller hearts, it makes more sense to use 226 minus age. Regardless of which equation you use, keep in mind that if you obtain the client's predicted maximum heart rate from an equation rather than from a maximal stress test conducted in a lab, it is only an estimate. One expert has suggested that these guesstimates can be as much as 11 beats per minute too high or too low for 30 percent of the population!

If you're primarily interested in promoting weight loss in a beginning exerciser, I suggest that you start with 60 percent of the MHR and eventually move up to 70 percent. These weight-loss CV workouts should last 40 to 60 minutes. Experienced exercisers who have established a base of conditioning and want to improve their cardiovascular fitness should aim for 70 to 80 percent of MHR. Clients seeking to improve athletic performance, for example, those who are planning to race in a local 10K race, need to do at least some of their CV training in the 80 percent or greater range. These should be interval sessions during which the client varies between very high and moderate intensity.

You should also encourage your client to monitor her rate of perceived exertion (RPE), a subjective measure of how hard she is working. On a 1 to 10 scale, 4 to 6 corresponds to 60 to 70 percent MHR, while 7 to 8 is more like 75 to 85 percent MHR. This type of monitoring can be surprisingly accurate. It also has the advantage of increasing your client's body awareness.

Duration

The lower the intensity of the exercise, the longer your client will be able to continue. Elderly, extremely overweight, or otherwise compromised clients will be unable to sustain anything beyond the lowest intensity activity for more than a very few minutes, and you might need to begin with less than the 20-minute minimum recommended by ACSM. If this is the case, your goal should be to maintain intensity while gradually increasing the number of minutes per session until your client can do 20 minutes nonstop. As mentioned above, eventually you'll want these clients to do sessions of 40 to 60 minutes at 60 to 70 percent of their MHR.

Appropriate Method

Obese, elderly, or poorly conditioned clients need to do low intensity cardiovascular exercise without any complicated movement patterns. Walking fills this bill perfectly, and is therefore usually the best form of cardiovascular exercise to recommend to them. Once a basic level of conditioning has been achieved, you should plan some higher intensity CV exercise for all clients. Some clients enjoy group activities, and might want to participate in an aerobics class. Others enjoy working out at home, and will be more likely to do CV exercise consistently if they purchase a piece of equipment (stationary bike, treadmill, or stairstepper) for the home. Discuss the factors with your client and come up with the method that he is most likely to do consistently. The best cardiovascular exercise for your client is the one that he likes enough (or at least finds tolerable enough) to do frequently.

Improving CV Programs

Have your clients keep logs of their cardiovascular exercise and review these logs periodically. When your client is progressing through the stages of conditioning, especially the very important improvement stage, it is essential to have the information on her energy levels, perceived exertion, and exercise heart rate that the log will provide. In addition, simply being accountable to the log, a surrogate you, will provide that needed nudge on days when your client is tempted to skip her time on the treadmill or exercise bike.

Make sure that the cardiovascular exercise you recommend is challenging, but not too difficult.

Obviously, you need to suggest that your client work hard enough to obtain the many benefits of cardiovascular exercise, but if you demand that he work to the point of exhaustion during every CV workout, he will dread doing it, eventually so much so that he will stop doing it altogether! It's better that your client work out consistently, even at a lower level of intensity, than only intend to work out, think about working out while he's lying on the couch, or otherwise avoid doing a routine that's difficult, painful, and makes him feel like a failure at a higher intensity. Have your client record both his rate of perceived exertion and exercise heart rate, and keep these in mind when you design your routines.

Be aware that boredom is a constant lurking danger with CV exercise, and suggest strategies to avoid it, including alternate types of exercise and even distractions such as reading (my personal favorite). Give your client the advantage of warning her that it's natural to be bored with CV exercise sometimes, and remind her that keeping the advantages in mind and varying the method will keep her on track. I find it helps some people do their CV workouts if they have some sort of distraction to keep them from getting bored. Reading, watching television, listening to music, even returning phone calls can keep your client on that bike for the full 30 minutes she needs.

I've also found that it's useful to have clients use heart monitors during their CV workouts. The purpose of using the heart monitor is not only to give the client a subjective feel for how hard he should be working during his workout, but also to give clients a gadget to play with, which some find motivating. Don't underestimate the effectiveness of gadgets in overcoming boredom. With some clients, this will make the difference between three CV sessions per week and three missed sessions.

The Flexibility Component

Flexibility is the ability of a joint to move through a range of motion. Despite the fact that it is widely believed that stretching reduces incidence of injury, there is scant research to back up this claim. Still, I feel it is important, especially as we age. It helps clients maintain good posture and enhances their body awareness. It is relaxing, and it feels good! Unfortunately, flexibility tends to be the aspect of fitness most often sacrificed to lack of time. Time-pressed clients congratulate themselves for consistently doing their aerobics and resistance training, and think, "Enough already! I have a life!" when it comes time to stretch. You can probably empathize with these feelings, but you should encourage your clients to stretch regularly, and you should include flexibility training as part of every (or almost every) session.

The best time for flexibility training is at the end, after the muscles are warmed up and their tightness, as well as that of the connective tissue, is reduced. *Never* stretch a cold muscle! This is asking for injury.

Discourage your clients from engaging in bouncing, or ballistic, stretches. As you know from your anatomy and physiology training, when a muscle is stretched too quickly, it tightens as a protective reflex. The body is making sure that the muscle does not get overstretched or torn. Suggest that your client take the muscle into a perceptible, but not painful, stretch and hold it for a minimum of 20

Benefits of CV Exercise
• Increase in $\dot{V}O_2$max
• Decrease in maximal and resting heart rate and increased stroke volume (more blood pumped per heartbeat)
• Decrease in body fat (assuming overall calorie deficit)
• Reduced blood pressure
• Increased HDL (good) cholesterol
• Improved glucose metabolism
• More efficient transport and utilization of oxygen
• Improved ability to burn fat

Stretching Guidelines
• Warm up before stretching.
• Hold stretches for at least 20 seconds, and preferably 30 to 60 seconds, or do each stretch three to four times and hold for 15 to 20 seconds.

• Avoid stretching without the prior consent of a physician if
  • you have a recent fracture or sprain,
  • you have suspected or diagnosed osteoporosis,
  • you have inflammation around a joint, or
  • you experience sharp, stabbing pain during stretching.

(preferably 30) seconds. I strongly recommend that you time these stretches. You'd be amazed how 30 seconds can seem like an eternity when you're holding a stretch, and if it doesn't seem like an eternity to you, it will to your client. I've noticed this distorted time sense is especially acute in beginning stretchers, I suspect because stretching feels so unnatural, and maybe almost painful. Reassure your client that stretching, like everything else you're doing together, will get easier, but not unless she holds the stretches at least 20 seconds. Some research suggests that four sets of 15 to 20 seconds per stretch will produce the greatest increases in flexibility.

Each joint has its own range of motion. Don't assume that a client with an extremely flexible upper body has equal flexibility in the low back and hamstrings. Also, remember that women tend to be more flexible than men, and well-conditioned clients more than sedentary people.

The Nutritional Component

As mentioned before, you must be cautious about giving advice about anything beyond your expertise, including nutrition. You should refrain from giving clients special diets that claim to treat disease or other medical problems. Limit your nutritional advice to general concepts of good nutrition. We want our clients to eat diets low in fat and high in complex carbohydrates. We also want them to consume alcohol and simple sugars such as honey, syrup, and candy only in moderation. In addition to explaining these guidelines, you can recommend books to your clients so that they can learn more about good nutrition. You should also consider networking with one or several registered dietitians to whom you can refer your clients and from whom you can get referrals.

CHAPTER 5

Individualized Program Design

Step 1: Evaluating and Screening Your Clients

A health history questionnaire will give you the information you need to screen your clients and determine which ones absolutely cannot begin your program without written permission from their physicians. (A sample health history questionnaire is included in appendix A.) You should recommend that all clients, even apparently healthy ones, see their doctors for checkups prior to beginning an exercise program. This is especially true of sedentary people over 40. I use American College of Sports Medicine guidelines to decide whether to require that a client obtain a written consent from a physician before beginning an exercise program.

The ACSM guidelines divide clients into three categories:

1. Apparently healthy, with the subcategories "younger" and "over 40 (men)" or "over 50 (women)"

2. Individuals at higher risk

3. Patients with disease

I strongly suggest that you consult ACSM's *Guidelines for Exercise Testing and Prescription* (5th ed.) (see Suggested Reading) for a more thorough understanding of these important screening criteria.

Occasionally, the answers you get on the health history questionnaire dictate that you decline to work with a particular client. Do not hesitate to refer a client with special needs to another trainer or other health professional (for example, a physical therapist or kinesiotherapist) who might be better able to help her. You do no one, especially yourself, a favor by taking on clients whose needs and challenges are beyond your knowledge and ability.

The Fitness Assessment

Why do you need to do a fitness assessment?

To Gather Information

Many people never begin an exercise program because they don't have a clue about where to begin. The answer is, of course, to begin at the beginning, which is wherever you are now. The fitness assessment tells you where the client is now in terms of his cardiovascular fitness, strength, and flexibility. It gives you the information you need to design a program that will condition all the major muscle groups, promote balance in every joint, and condition the heart and lungs. It gives you a record you can look back at to see that you have accomplished your goals. It shows you where your client is and where you want to go together.

To Focus on Objectives

Good program design requires a thoughtful, careful analysis of the methods, reasons, and manner of each exercise or protocol. The fitness assessment helps you answer these what's-the-point questions about your client's program. For example, if a client is in excellent cardiovascular condition, but is too weak to carry in a medium-sized bag of groceries, you know that you need to focus on improving strength.

To Motivate the Client

One of the strongest motivators to continue a program is seeing progress. How can you show your client that he has made progress if you don't have a record of where he started?

To Detect Special Fitness Needs

In my experience, most adults have tightness in the neck, shoulders (especially the internal rotators), low back, and hamstrings. Your client might be the exception to this general rule. If she's not, though, you need to know about it. You also need to know if she stands with a swaybacked posture, if her toes point out excessively (think of Charlie Chaplin), or if one hip is higher than the other. Why? Back pain, twinges in the hip, and achy neck and shoulders can often be attributed to bad posture or structural asymmetry. You need to know which muscles need to be strengthened and stretched to correct these problems and help your client achieve optimal balance and function.

> Most people find it difficult to continue doing anything that they find extremely uncomfortable or feel awkward doing. Many previously sedentary people fear beginning a program in the first place for just this reason. If you know your client's fitness level, you can design a program that will be challenging, but achievable. Your client will experience success and positive reinforcement, and be highly motivated to continue exercising.

To Design a Realistic Program

It's difficult to say which has caused more human misery, good intentions or the unrealistic expectations they create. Compare these two clients, who both begin a three-month program with you. The first expects to lose 40 pounds and 15 percent body fat. The second expects to lose 10 pounds and 5 percent body fat. Both lose 15 pounds and 7 percent body fat. Which client do you think will be happier? Which will be disappointed, perhaps so disappointed that she will conclude that she's been working for nothing?

The Body Composition Test

Clients tend to feel about body composition tests the way many of us feel about IQ tests: We have an

---

Do You Need to Do Every Test on Every Client?

The short answer is no, of course not! If, for example, you're working with a well-conditioned weightlifter who wants your help increasing the strength and flexibility of his rotator cuff, you might not do a cardiovascular fitness test or a body composition test. There are clients whose medical histories dictate that they avoid any cardiovascular testing outside of a medically supervised environment. This is a judgment call, but as always, err on the conservative side. If you have any doubts about whether to do a particular test on a client, don't do it without consulting the client's physician. Some clients with no medical limitations will specifically request that you not ask them to do a particular test, and since they are ultimately in control of this whole process, that's their choice. You should explain why you think it's advisable to do the testing, but if they decline, proceed cautiously, even more than you normally would with someone of this age, gender, and medical and exercise history. Specifics on performing the fitness tests are contained in appendix B.

---

almost irresistible impulse to know the result, an uneasiness about the possibility that the result might not be as good as we hope, and a terror of anyone else finding out. I can say without hesitation that every single client you work with will want to know what his or her body fat percentage is after you explain the concept of body composition, lean weight versus fat weight, and the insignificance of the number of pounds he or she weighs. I also guarantee that clients will fear the result. In fact, some clients approach these tests with sheer terror. You need to recognize that for these clients, seeing what they consider the "wrong" number in this test result is a crushing personal failure. Try to avoid this counterproductive reaction by explaining the real, rather than imagined, implications of the test, how what you're really measuring is a *range* within which her body fat falls, and how uncontrollable variables unrelated to body fat (water retention, for example) can affect the result. If your client understands that a few millimeters difference in a skinfold measurement can show up as a five percent difference on a body composition test, it's less likely that she will spend any time crying over the result. (Yes, I've had clients cry over the results of their body fat tests!)

I suggest that you measure subcutaneous body fat (the body fat directly under the skin, as opposed to intramuscular fat) with calipers and take measurements with a tape measure. Specific instructions on performing the body fat tests and tables for interpreting them are contained in the reference books in Suggested Reading. To compute body fat percentage, see appendix B, pages 167-168.

Flexibility Tests

As I mentioned previously, you should encourage your clients to work on their flexibility as well as other aspects of fitness. To find out where your clients are starting from, I suggest that you do two flexibility tests on all of them, the sit-and-reach test and the finger-touch test (page 169 in appendix B). I selected these because they address the two areas that are problems for most adults: the hamstrings and the rotator cuffs. Remember that flexibility is joint specific. A person can be like Gumby when it comes to his hamstrings, yet have such tight rotator cuffs that he looks like the Hunchback of Notre Dame!

Suggested Tests to Perform During Your Clients' Fitness Assessments
• Height
• Weight
• Blood pressure
• Resting pulse
• Body composition
• Anthropometric measurements
• Sit-and-reach test
• Finger-touch test
• Curl-up test
• Push-up test
• Posture evaluation

Cardiovascular Fitness Tests

Cardiovascular fitness can be measured in many ways, some more accurate than others. The most accurate tests are done in sports medicine labs or clinics and involve expensive, bulky equipment. While these tests will give the most accurate results, you can do the 3-minute step test described in appendix B without costly equipment to measure your client's cardiovascular fitness.

Evaluating Posture and Muscular Imbalance

Good posture is functional posture. It is a natural body alignment that allows you to move in a pain free, efficient way. Unfortunately, many of us develop bad posture early in life and spend the next several decades cementing our joints in these misshapen twists and warps. Overcoming bad posture requires identifying the problem and taking corrective action, stretching the shortened structures and strengthening the opposing muscle groups. In my experience, the overwhelming majority of adults suffer from some very common postural deficiencies. The typical new client that I see has rounded shoulders, a tight, almost spasmodic neck, and a hanging head. Often these conditions are accompanied by other dysfunctional conditions: locked knees, outward-pointing toes, and lordosis, commonly known as swayback, which is an exaggerated forward curvature of the spine that causes the stomach to stick out and the low back to arch excessively. Others have kneecaps that turn in toward each other, usually due to tight hip rotators.

"A steady and pleasant posture produces mental equilibrium and prevents fickleness of mind."

B.K.S. Iyengar, noted yoga master

Visual Inspection

Many of us, confronted with our less-than-exemplary posture, react to this reminder as if we've been zapped with an unexpected bolt of electricity, hyperarching our backs into exaggerated military contortions that would embarrass a corps of West Point cadets. To avoid this reaction, evaluate your client's posture without comment. Do the following posture check to see where she stands.

Hang-dog head: We spend so much time looking down that we often fall into the habit of walking around looking down. Not only does this make you look like you lost your last friend, it causes enormous stress in the muscles of the neck and upper back as they struggle to hold up the weight of the head and keep the chin off the chest. These muscles were never intended to do this task, and like any workers forced to do jobs outside their job descriptions, they complain loudly and frequently until this condition is corrected. Hang-dog head often goes in tandem with lordosis and excessively pointed toes.

As the body tries to bring the head into alignment with the lower spine, which, when these conditions are present, is out of functional alignment, it puts the head in a contorted and inappropriate position.

Shoulder at 1 o'clock, not 12 o'clock: Ask your client to visualize his shoulder from the side as the face of a clock. The top of this clock face (12 o'clock) should align with the end of the collarbone. It should not point forward (1 o'clock).

Four-finger space: Does your client have her rib cage lifted up and out from the pelvis with an identifiable space between her pelvis and rib cage, or is she slouching so that you can barely slide a sheet of paper in between them?

Winging scapula: Is your client's scapula flat against his spine or is there a palpable space, almost like a little vertical shelf, where his scapula sticks out?

Swayback: As mentioned before, this is known by the scary name lordosis, but by any name, it's a major problem. It can cause low back pain and sciatica (pain in the legs caused by pressure on nerves), not to mention making your belly stick out in front like you're carrying a sack of dirty sweatsocks. The derriere sticks out in back like a shelf attached to your low spine. This is caused by the pelvis tilting forward, out of its proper alignment.

Locked knees: If a person stands with her knees locked, two things are happening—the knees are not serving the shock absorption function that they should under ideal circumstances, and the person is not using the powerful muscles in her legs to move. If knees are locked, walking is initiated at the hip and the quadriceps and hamstrings are not functioning as they should.

Excessively pointed toes: Often related to swayback, hanging head, and round shoulders, walking with your feet out like Charlie Chaplin's Little Tramp character can cause pain in hips, knees, and ankles.

Sagging ankles: Are the ankles straight and directly below the knees, or do they cave in?

Compensation and Pain

Pain is a symptom of a problem. So is moving in an unnatural manner to avoid pain that you know will result if you move normally. Ask your clients about pain during their daily activities. You might discover things about their work habits, work stations, or other activities that are causing problems that you need to address, either directly or by referral to another appropriate health professional. It might be obvious to you which muscles need to be stretched and strengthened to correct the conditions you observe. If not, suggest that your client consult with a physician, physical therapist, or other qualified health professional. Don't try to treat conditions beyond your knowledge or ability.

> Advise your client that she should feel free to stop exercising any time she feels dizziness, lightheadedness, chest pain, or nausea, or for any other reason.

Perfect Posture

Now that I've told you all about posture dysfunctions, how will you know perfect posture when you see it? Look for the following:

- Head erect, floating on the spinal column
- Four-finger space between rib cage and pelvis
- Shoulder joints in line with hip joints
- Shoulders level
- Shoulder blades depressed
- Hands at the sides, not with backs of the hands facing front
- Hips level
- Abdominals contracted to hold the pelvis in proper alignment
- Kneecaps directly over feet, not pointing inward
- Knees soft, not locked
- Feet pointing forward

Step 2: Consider Client Preferences and Limitations

It is much more likely that your client will exercise consistently and effectively if she

- feels she has been a part of the process of program design,
- feels her particular special needs, if any, have been taken into account, and
- isn't required to do anything that she really despises.

Try to facilitate your client's workouts by making them as convenient as possible. Walking after work instead of driving to the club might be more palatable to your client. Another helpful suggestion: If she needs to do more CV exercise and lives in a cold climate, suggest that she invest in a piece of indoor equipment, pointing out how unlikely it is that she'll go out in the dark on a 10-below January day to do that power walk.

Step 3:
Set Objectives That Are TOPS

What are TOPS objectives?

- **T**imed—Set a target date for reaching each goal.

- **O**bjective—A measurable goal is meaningful precisely because you can tell when you have reached it. Don't say "get leaner." Instead, say "Reduce body fat by .5 percent each month."

- **P**ersonalized—In addition to general overall fitness goals that most clients have, like reducing body fat percentages, your client probably has some specific things he'd like to work on. For example, he might be planning a spring ski trip and need some specific attention to pre-ski conditioning. You need to include this in your goals.

- **S**pecific—Making the goals as specific as you can will encourage your client by giving him a clear objective.

Step 4:
Select Appropriate Cardiovascular Protocol

Consider each client's unique situation.

Step 5:
Select Resistance Training Exercise

Consider: Weights or machines? Home or gym?

Step 6:
Write the Program

Include "homework" (any activities that you want your client to do between your sessions as described in chapter 6) and the flexibility training.

Step 7:
Set the Time Parameters

Set realistic parameters for achieving specific goals in each area.

Step 8:
Determine Progress

Goals should be measured daily, weekly, and monthly.

Now you're ready to put it all together: the ultimate, top-of-the-mountain goal, and all the plateaus along the way. Chapter 8 contains a sample goal map setting out these short-, intermediate-, and long-term goals.

Writing the Program—A Checklist

- Did you do a thorough fitness assessment? If not, why not?
- Has your client completed a health history questionnaire?
- If your client's condition dictates that you do so, have you obtained a signed medical clearance from his doctor?
- Has your client completed a goal inventory?
- Do you understand your client's goals and objectives?
- Have you discussed realistic goals?
- Have you considered this client's special needs and limitations, both physiological (diabetes, hypertension, or obesity, for example) and orthopedic (e.g., low back, shoulder, or knee problems or arthritis)?
- Have you recommended that your client learn about nutrition, especially the benefits of a low-fat, low-sugar diet?
- Have you taken into account the available time and equipment?
- Is the workout one that your client can complete in a reasonable (less than one hour) amount of time?
- Have you examined your client's attitudes toward exercise in general and toward specific activities?
- Have you discussed the general benefits of exercise with your client?
- Have you explained the objectives of the program to your client?
- Have you included two to three resistance training workouts per week for every major muscle group, in the 8 to 12 repetition range, unless otherwise dictated by this client's needs?
- Is your resistance routine balanced, that is, does it work opposing muscle groups for balance around each joint?
- Have you included three to five cardiovascular workouts of 20 to 60 minutes duration at 55 to 80 percent of the client's maximal heart rate in each week's routine?
- Have you included flexibility exercises and taught your client how to do them?
- Have you included stretching and muscle balance exercises for the low back and rotator cuffs?
- Have you established timed, objective, personalized, specific goals in the areas of body composition, cardiovascular fitness, muscular strength, and flexibility?
- Have you set a date for retesting?
- Have you discussed "homework" with your client, that is, the activity, time, and intensity of the workouts he should do between sessions with you?
- Have you kept the client's overall life in mind, making sure that the workout is realistic and doable for him?
- Have you designed a workout that your client will actually do on a regular basis, one that is challenging enough to improve his energy, fitness, and overall well-being, but isn't so difficult he will dread doing it and eventually stop doing it altogether?

CHAPTER 6

Conducting the Workout

When you begin working with a new client, you should set up a record book for her. I use three-ring notebooks containing the following:

- workout record forms (see appendix A) and
- copies of goal inventories, homework, and related materials that you have given your client.

Plan Everything

Before the scheduled session, you should plan everything about the workout—the exercises, sets, and reps, basing your plan on your previous experience with this client, or if this is your first workout together, your best estimate based on the results of your fitness assessment. Remember to *always* err on the conservative side! You can increase the amount of weight or number of reps on the second or third set if necessary. Make a habit of noting these adjustments in the workout record. Then before you begin, determine whether any of the information you got in this pre-exercise exchange dictates that you should change any aspect of the planned workout. Be flexible in your plan. When you arrive at the session, circumstances could require that you change everything. What if you have an upper-body workout planned, but your client tells you when you arrive that she hurt her wrist? You might have to change everything, and you should be prepared to do so.

The Warm-Up

Sometimes clients will arrive late for a workout. "C'mon—do I have to warm up?" they plead. "Let's

Before beginning a workout (including the warm-up), go over the MAPP. After exchanging pleasantries when you greet the client, always ask
• Are you taking **M**edication?
• Do you have any **A**ches that might affect your ability to exercise?
• Do you have any **P**ain, and if so, where?
• Do you have any other **P**roblems that might affect your workout?

just get started." It is at this point that my ability to tell people things they don't want to hear comes in quite handy. A general warm-up is essential prior to beginning the workout. It decreases the risk of injury by raising muscle temperature, thereby making them contract more efficiently. It makes muscles more pliable. It reduces the risk of tearing tendons and ligaments. It increases blood flow to working muscle.

Now that I've convinced you that a warm-up is essential and provided you with ammunition to combat your clients' protestations that they don't have time to warm up, please understand that you don't need to overdo it. You don't want your client so wiped out by the warm-up that he is unable to do a single resistance exercise. I recommend a minimum of five minutes of moderate CV exercise, usually on a stationary bike, before beginning the workout. You can tell that the client is warmed up when he breaks a sweat.

In addition to the general warm-up, you should have your client do a specific warm-up for the muscle or muscle groups being worked with approximately 50 percent of the weight of the first set prior to working it. This warm-up set is especially important for exercises involving the knee, low back, and shoulder.

The Resistance Portion of the Workout

After your client has completed his general warm-up, it's time to head for the weights (or machines, bands, or other equipment) and take him through the resistance exercises that you have planned.

The first few times you do an exercise with a client, and periodically thereafter, you should explain all of the following:

- The name of the exercise (Your clients probably won't remember most of these names. Everytime you say "seated dumbbell triceps extension," your client will say, "You mean dumbbell behind the head?")
- The muscle or muscle groups being worked
- The muscle or muscle group's function
- The pivot point
- Body position and correct center of gravity
- Form points
- Common mistakes in form made by beginners

Yes, SIR – That Set Was Tough!

After each set, it's useful to ask the client how difficult the set was for her to complete. You can use these responses to decide whether to decrease the rest interval or increase reps or weight, or even to determine whether your client feels the muscles contracting the way she should. Rather than simply asking, "How hard was that?" and having the client say, "Not too bad," or "Really horrible," I've found I can get a much more specific, informative response by asking, "On a scale of 1 to 10, if 1 is like lying on the couch watching X Files and 10 is like trying to lift the Sears Tower, how would you rate the difficulty of that last set?" I call this the client's subjective intensity rating (SIR) for this set. Record these for each set, or at least for the last set of each exercise. When you do your postsession review, use these numbers to plan the next session.

Subjective Intensity Rating (SIR)

1	Like lying on the couch watching X Files
2 to 3	The effort required to walk to the fridge
4 to 5	Almost broke a sweat
6	Moderately challenging
7 to 8	Last two or three reps were really tough
9	Like trying to give a piggyback ride to a Sumo wrestler
10	Like trying to lift the Sears Tower

In most cases, you want clients to rate the exercise in the 7 to 8 area.

The Cool-Down and Flexibility Training Portions of the Workout

The cool-down portion of a cardiovascular session consists of slow, low intensity (30 to 40 percent MHR) activity such as pedaling with low or no resistance or slow treadmill walking. The cool-down helps prevent venous blood pooling and lowers the probability of cardiac arrhythmias. It's easy to understand why when you remember that during exercise the contracting muscles help to move blood back to the heart. When you stop exercising, blood can tend to "pool" in the extremities, which can cause blood pressure to drop and even irregular heartbeat or arrhythmia. Be sure to explain the importance of cool-down to your client since he will probably be working out on his own, at least from time to time.

Since it's not advisable to stretch when muscles are cold, stretch after the workout when they are warmed up and in optimal stretching condition. (If your client prefers, he may stretch after his general warm-up, but never before!) If your workout with your client consists of resistance training only, stretching will serve as the cool-down portion. Plan the flexibility training so that you give priority to joints that need the most work. Remember that when it comes to stretching, halfway is no way. If you don't hold a stretch long enough, it does not improve flexibility and range of motion in the joint. When you're stretching, especially stretching joints that have limited range of motion, 20 to 30 seconds will seem like forever, and your normally astute sense of time will desert you, so time the length that your client holds his stretches and use these prolonged intervals to check proper form. On especially tight areas, it's advisable to perform each stretch three to five times and to include stretches for these areas in the client's homework. See the Resistance Workout Guide for stretches for particular muscles and joints.

The Reinforcing Good-Bye

There are some clients you will see only once a week, once every two weeks, or once a month. With these clients, it's important that you send them off with praise for their successes during today's workout and specific instructions about what they need to do before your next session.

Positive Feedback and Reinforcement

Find something positive about your client's performance and point it out. If her form on an exercise you've been working on has improved, tell her! Say it loud, say it proud! Sometimes we assume that our clients know that they're improving, but we forget the natural human tendency to discount improvement and focus on the things that aren't getting better.

> Praise their successes!

Homework

I like to assign my clients specific activities to do before our next session. For beginners, often it is only their cardiovascular sessions and stretching, but even in these cases, I give them a target time and intensity and a list of stretches to do. More advanced clients get more detailed workouts with specific exercises, sets, reps, and rest intervals. Be sure to explain everything that you give a client to do on his own! Never assume that he understands what he is supposed to do just because you've done it together a hundred times. Often clients suffer from sensory overload during your workouts together, and when left on their own, their memories of the specifics are as fuzzy as a well-worn polyester shirt.

The Session Doesn't End When the Client Leaves

After the session, go over your notes, client SIRs for each exercise, and your overall annual, semiannual, or quarterly plan for this client. Make additional notes about specific areas you want to work on at the next session or subsequent sessions.

Keep Accurate Records

There will come a day when your client will ask, "How much weight did I use the first time I did a bench press?" or, "What's the most I've ever done on the leg press?" Your client might also tell you that his right knee has been very sore for about three days and ask you why. You've got to be able to answer these questions, not only to be responsive to your client, but also because information about your client's progress is vital in designing his program. Sometimes it's hard to remember to write everything down while you're trying to talk to your client, watch his form, and focus on the workout, but it's very important to do so. You should write down any aches, pains, or problems at the beginning before you begin the workout. As for keeping track of the volume of work, the best way to make sure you keep an accurate record is to write down the number of reps after each set. By the way, counting reps is important. Sometimes when you're trying to watch your client's form, correct mistakes, and give encouragement, you tend to lose count; therefore, you might suggest to the client that he count, too, or give him a target number of reps so that he can let you know when he gets there. A sample workout record form is provided in appendix A.

Each workout is more than just another day at the office. At the end of several weeks or months, when you both look at the transformation that has occurred and celebrate your achievements, recall that it happened one workout at at time. So approach each session as the important thing it is: a small step toward the goals that you and your client have determined to reach.

CHAPTER 7

Conducting Yourself

Be a Good Citizen—Follow the Rules

There are some rules of gym etiquette—good manners for the weight room—that are known to bodybuilders and weight trainers throughout the world. You should always try to comply with these standards when you are working with clients. Being a good gym "citizen" will make the experience more pleasant not only for you and the client but also for other gym members. Keep in mind that your client will probably be someone who hasn't spent any time in a gym and who looks to you to set an example about how to behave. Make sure you set a good one. These, then, are the "rules."

Respect Other Members

When you approach a bench with a towel on it, or a pair of dumbbells resting on the floor nearby, or other evidence that suggests that someone might be returning to finish a set, ask people standing around if anyone is working there. Few things are more annoying to weight trainers than their fellow gym members just walking up and taking over their spot or the equipment they're using. Always ask. Often several people will be using a particular piece of equipment, so you'll have to be courteous and work in (see below) with other gym members.

Politely Ask to Work In

The custom of *working in* is accepted in weight rooms all over the world (really—I once worked in with someone in Japan). In case you're unfamiliar with the term, working in means using a piece of equipment while another gym member is resting between sets. Let's say you're working with your client Nancy Novice and you want to use the 10-pound dumbbells. Unfortunately, as you approach the weight area, you discover that someone else is using them. Waiting until she is finished with her set, you say politely, "Is it OK if she (indicating your client) works in with you with the 10s?" Ninety-nine point nine percent of the time the person will smile and say "yes." When he or she doesn't, you're probably dealing with a dysfunctional person.

Beware of Rude People

Every gym, school, and workplace has some of these. Unfortunately, gyms may have more than their share because of the hideous and well-documented psychological side effects of anabolic steroids. Once you are around a particular gym or club for a while, you will get to know who these people are. They're the ones who strut around as if they own the place, bellowing unsolicited comments about other members and anything else that enters their minds. They don't converse so much as broadcast their opinionated bleating to the entire room. In my experience, some of these people find your very presence a threat. After all, why should a client hire you to get advice on exercise when she could just ask him? He's a lot more muscular than you'll ever be, right? If you have the misfortune to encounter one of these individuals, understand that they live in their own world. If they're rude to you, resist the temptation to respond in kind by telling them to put it where the sun don't shine. Remember that you are a professional and you have your client to think of. A confrontation will only make you look bad. Just get your client out of harm's way.

Clubs and gyms don't want troublemakers either. So make a note of exactly what happened or was said in any untoward incident and inform the gym's management in writing, being very specific: Documentation may come in handy.

Be Friendly

One of the reasons your client likes working with you is that you are a friendly, pleasant person. Your client will appreciate your being friendly and polite to other gym members, too. Introduce yourself to other members and learn their names. Saying "Hi, Steve. Mind if she works in with you here?" instead of "Hey you—can we work in?" will smooth the way for your client.

Help Your Client Get Acclimated to the Gym Environment

It may come as a surprise to you, since you find the clanging of barbells and the grunts and groans of sweaty hulks as natural as breathing, to learn that many clients will feel as out of place in this environment as they would at a stag party in Sunday school. I can remember a client, previously a very sedentary, middle-aged woman, whose eyes grew as large as saucers the first time she saw—and, more importantly, heard—a tattooed young man struggle and strain doing battle with a pair of 100-pounders. He had barely completed his last rep when, with a triumphant cry, he allowed the dumbbells to crash to the floor. She visibly slumped, as if trying to hide from what clearly was a frightening situation. If you put yourself in her place, her feelings won't seem that unusual. Have empathy for your client, and try to make her feel at home in the gym. Introduce her to fellow members that you know, and explain that those guys, scary as they look and sound, are really harmless.

Mind Your Own Business

A day never passes that I don't see things in the gym that give me nightmares. Some of the gyrations that pass for proper form are injuries waiting to happen. In law, there is a term called the *officious intermeddler*, defined as someone who sticks his nose in a situation without invitation. I won't bore you with a bunch of legal mumbo-jumbo. Suffice it to say that almost no one appreciates unsolicited advice, no matter how good it is. Be like me: Walk around with little red teeth marks on your lip, but say nothing.

Avoid Distractions

During and immediately after the workout, your attention must remain riveted on your client. If you do a lot of your workouts in the same gym or club, you'll get to know lots of people there, and while being friendly is always a good policy, don't let your desire to be sociable interfere with your number one priority, your client. For example, don't get caught up in a conversation with another gym member and leave your client left out, standing around awkwardly wondering what to do next, wondering whether you've forgotten he is there, and wondering why he is working with you in the first place! After saying hello, introducing your client by name to your gym pal, excuse yourself and move to the next exercise.

Get There First, or the Importance of Punctuality

How many times have you been late for something because a semi jackknifed and spilled frozen green beans all over the expressway, a 300-car freight train was between you and your destination, or some similar catastrophe? When a client is waiting for you, even one time is too many. *Never* be late for a workout! Always assume that some unforeseen event beyond your control is going to happen and leave 5 to 10 minutes earlier than you think you have to. If you're going to a new place, I suggest that you drive there in advance two or three days before the scheduled appointment and figure out the best way to get there and just how long it takes. Then you won't be surprised, or more important, late. Oh, and one more thing: When you schedule your day like this, you will probably arrive before the client. That's ideal because it gives you time to go over the workout again, think about the specific instructions you're going to give the client during the workout, and generally be well-prepared.

Never be late for a workout!

Special Considerations of Home Workouts

Home workouts have become quite popular, as the vast assortment of home fitness equipment will attest. It's no wonder. The convenience of home workouts is tough to beat. The only downside for some would-be fitness buffs is the lack of knowledgeable instructors. That's where you come in. When someone invites you into her home, even as a paid professional, she is making a statement about the confidence she has in you. Let's face it: Most of us wouldn't let just anyone into our homes. It's a special trust, one placed in you because of your professionalism and competence. Of course, going into a client's home is much like going into anyone else's home—good manners are always in style. In your capacity as a professional, there are some other things to think of.

Never enter a client's home without permission. Sometimes clients will tell you that they will leave the door open for you when you come, and in these cases, of course you should let yourself in. Until your client tells you this, though, you should always just ring the doorbell and wait patiently to be let in. If you knock on the door and ring the doorbell and get no answer, be sure to leave a note in the door, stating you were there and saying that you're sorry you missed her. Go out to the car, phone and leave a message on the machine, then wait five minutes in your car before leaving. While this happens rarely, it's important that the client know that you did show up when you were supposed to.

It's desirable, but not essential, that the phone be in the same room that you and the client are using to workout. If not, make sure that it's accessible to you in case of an emergency. Yes, sometimes clients look twice at you when you say, "OK, before we get started, I need to know where the phone is, and whether this area is served by a 911 system." Be prepared for your client to look a little disconcerted and say, "Why? Are you going to push me until I

have a heart attack?" They feel quite reassured when you reply that even though you've never hurt anyone, you want to be prepared for any contingency.

Treat your client's furniture with special care. If she offers you something to drink, be sure to use a coaster before placing a glass on a table. You may have to ask for one, and she may say, "Oh, you don't have to use a coaster on that table. It's from a garage sale," but make sure you ask first.

Ensure that the workout area is safe; that is, that there is no loose carpet, water, extension cord, or other object or condition that might cause your client (or anyone else in the area, for that matter) to slip and fall. As you complete an exercise, pick up and put away equipment. Don't leave the area littered with objects.

Children

During your initial consultation, talk to your client about how you can ensure that you have an hour of uninterrupted time for the workouts. Often stay-at-home parents can find this hour while their children are at school or napping. The important thing is to make sure that the client can concentrate on working out without worrying about having to drop everything to deal with children. Once the importance of being able to focus on the workout is explained, this isn't usually a problem. What can sometimes be a problem is children coming into the workout area and causing a potentially dangerous situation. We try to minimize this risk by suggesting that the client keep the workout area off limits to children during the workout. Sometimes clients assure us that their children have been instructed about safety in the workout area, stay there all the time while they are working out, and that their presence won't cause any problems. In these cases, you should permit the children to stay, but use extra caution about moving bars and weights. Before you begin an exercise, check on the children's locations and advise them to stay out of the way. With children, it's especially important that you pick things up and keep the area reasonably clear of potential trip-over hazards. If the situation becomes dangerous, you will have to discuss it with the client before continuing with your workouts.

Pets

Many clients have pets, usually cats and dogs. You probably won't have to deal with them much, other

---

The first time you go to a client's home, be sure to get the following information:

- The location of the phone
- Whether the town or village is on a 911 system, and if not, the phone number for emergency medical service

than petting them if they greet you at the door. (Like every other general rule, this one has its exceptions. I remember the time when one client's three huge dogs got a bit testy with one another, and eventually ended up in a teeth-bared, snarling fight! Or the time I rescued a client's dog by dislodging a plastic toy from his throat. Or the time a client's dog got a tad frisky and bit me, unintentionally I think. In all cases, everything turned out fine, I'm happy to report!) If you and your client have agreed that you let yourself in, be sure that the door is closed behind you and that all pets are present and accounted for before you leave the entryway.

Be cautious conducting workouts in the presence of pets. Always know where they are before you move equipment or begin an exercise. A rambunctious dog underfoot adds nothing to a workout, except maybe an injury and a lawsuit!

In the introduction to this book, I told you that details would separate you from the pack and let everyone know that you are a professional. The little pearls in this chapter are examples of what I was talking about: They may seem like small things, but your clients will notice and marvel to their friends at being able to find a treasure like you!

CHAPTER 8

Motivating Your Client

Maintaining your clients' motivation to exercise is one of the biggest challenges you will have. Let's face it: You can't be with them every single day. (Even if a client could afford this, he probably would tire of it in a very short time.) Motivation must come from within. Each client will have his own reasons for beginning and staying with your program. Many are motivated by the desire to change their looks. Some want to improve their health or avoid lifestyle-related diseases. Others may need to relieve stress. Understanding why your client called you in the first place and what he expects to get from your program will help you design a program that addresses his needs, values, and expectations—in short, a program that he will stick with.

One Person's Emerald Is Another Person's Chartreuse: Understanding Your Client's Personal Motivation

If I ask you to picture the color "green," do you see the same thing I see? We use the word to communicate a description of a color, but say it to 10 people, and they might have 10 different pictures in their heads of what it means. Similarly, it might seem that almost every client who calls you is interested in one thing, and only one thing: losing weight. Getting in shape is a close second. What do statements really mean, anyway? When a client tells me that she wants to lose weight, I've been known to reply, "A person could lose a lot of weight in a hurry by cutting off one

of her legs, but I'm not sure that she would be much better off, are you?" Of course, this is ridiculous, but I think it makes the point. Your client doesn't really want to lose weight. She wants to change her body composition, to have more lean tissue and less fat. "Getting in shape" usually means the same thing to her. At least that's what I think she means, but what I think isn't important: What she thinks is. Push your clients to be specific about what they desire and what they expect (not always the same thing) from the program.

A key to providing targeted motivation to clients is understanding what they believe about their own abilities, exercise, and fitness level and what they value. Psychologists speak of the concept of *outcome expectancy*, the belief that something will lead to a desirable, valued outcome. In order to sustain your client's motivation, you will need to keep him focused on something he values and educate him about his ability to get it by continuing the program. Some clients have no doubt that exercise can do all of the wonderful things that you say it can, but don't believe that they can do it. ("Me, an athlete? What a laugh! I've been uncoordinated and unathletic my whole life!") These people need more work on bolstering their self-confidence about their ability to do the things you tell them they need to do. Create simple, very small goals that present opportunities for success. Build on these successes to eradicate their former impressions of themselves. Other clients need education about the benefits of exercise and good nutrition. They may not know, for example, that exercise can reduce their risk of adult-onset diabetes or stroke. For these clients, who have no interest in looking "buff," motivation comes from understanding that the payoff is long-term good health and independence. The bottom line: Tailor your motivation strategy to your clients' beliefs and values.

Goal Setting

You know that your clients look to you for inspiration, knowledge, encouragement, and most of all—results! You might say that results are like one Supreme Court justice's memorable comment about obscenity: You know them when you see them. This approach might seem tempting at first because it frees you of the responsibility of doing the hard work that is really the essence of professionalism in every field, that is, thinking and planning. Personal training is no exception. Like any professional, you will not be able to escape responsibility if your client doesn't achieve whatever constitutes results to him.

"If you don't know where you're going, you might end up where you are headed."
Dr. Rod Gilbert, sport psychologist

Setting specific, measurable, realistic goals for your client is an indispensable part of your job. Often clients come to us with a vague, poorly defined idea of what they hope to get from working with a personal trainer. Unless we help our clients focus their attention on specifically where they want to go, we are little more than glorified spotters.

Why Are Goals So Important?

Most people pay lip service to setting goals in all areas of life, but few have given much thought to why goal setting is important. In my years of working with clients, I have discovered that goal setting is a fundamental part of personal training. Here's a list of some of the benefits you can get from effective goal setting.

Make Overwhelming Tasks Manageable

Anyone who has run a marathon knows it's a lot easier to envision running one more mile (or in that last five, one more block), than to think of running the full 26.2. If your client needs to lose 15 pounds, you want to take her attention off losing the whole 15, especially if she has failed to do so in the past.

Rather, get her to think in terms of losing one pound a week for the first three weeks. As Robert Schuller often says, "By the yard, it's hard, but inch by inch, it's a cinch."

Clarify What Your Program Will and Won't Do

Many clients who ask us to help them get in shape don't have extensive knowledge about the risks and benefits of exercise or realize that exercise adaptations are very specific. You would not want your client, the Masters swimmer, to be surprised to discover that weight training will not improve his time in the 800-meter. If improving performance in his sport is a high priority for him, you should discover this in your initial goal setting conferences. With this information, you can not only design a better program, but clarify your client's expectations.

Create Realistic Expectations About Progress

One question we usually get from new clients is "When will I see results?" This is a golden opportunity to explain the best result he can hope for and the fact that results are a function of compliance with the program. For example, speaking to a woman who has come to you to get in shape for a Christmas trip to Hawaii, you might say something like this: "If you consistently stick 100 percent to the number of workouts per week and the nutrition plan we discussed, you should be able to lose .5 to 1 percent body fat per month. By your trip to Hawaii next Christmas, that would have you down to the 22 percent body fat goal we set. If you can't manage to stick to the whole program 100 percent of the time, your results will reflect that. We'll be checking your progress every month, so we can see if we need to make any adjustments to help you get in bikini shape in time." Trust me: Nothing sours someone on a program like unrealistic, and therefore unmet, expectations.

Provide a Structure to Keep Your Client on Track

People today are so deluged with information about exercise and nutrition that they often feel overwhelmed, ready to throw up their hands and scream, "I give up!" The goals you and your client set will help combat this feeling by giving her specific actions to take every day, week, and month to stay on track.

Process Goals and Outcome Goals

I work with my clients to define two types of goals: process goals and outcome goals. Think of these as means and ends. The process goals are the means. They are the map, the path you take to get to your destination. Outcome goals are just that—the ends, the destination.

The Goal Setting Process

These days goal setting has become almost a cliche, more blah blah blah from helmet-headed "gurus" in late night infomercials. That's a shame, because nearly every important accomplishment begins as a goal. A wise person once said that a goal is a dream with a deadline. That definition is an especially good one for fitness goals, which should be measurable and specific.

Step 1: Find Your Client's Fitness Dream

Notice that previously I said that I work with my clients to define their goals. Goal setting must be a team effort. The client's input is key. He must feel that he has a personal stake in both the process and the outcome. Otherwise, he won't be able to sustain the commitment necessary to stick with his program during the inevitable plateaus and even occasional setbacks.

We begin by getting the client to focus on his fitness dream. What is his idea of ultimate fitness? What was the vision that brought him to you in the first place? The goal inventory helps your client gather his thoughts (see page 160). I have found it useful to send these forms to clients in advance so that they can take the time to sit down in a quiet room and think before responding. After he has filled it out, go over it with him. During this conference, encourage your client to talk. And I mean really talk! Long, rambling, stream-of-consciousness monologues are fine. By listening, you'll learn a lot about your client, not only what he wants to accomplish, but his personality and his attitude about exercise. Does he seem like a driven, compulsive, list-making Type-A, or a more laid-back sort? What impression do you get of his commitment to making lifestyle changes?

After listening to your client describe his fitness dreams, it's time for you to narrow the focus from the global and general to the narrow and specific by asking the right questions. We want the client to

Your client needs to think about and answer these questions:
• What do I want to accomplish?
• Why do I want to accomplish this goal?
• Am I willing to pay the price?

understand the lifestyle changes he will have to make to reach his goals and to do a cost-benefit analysis. There's nothing like being hanged in the morning to focus a man's attention, and there's nothing like hearing that he will have to give up alcohol and desserts for the next 12 weeks to make him re-evaluate whether he really wants that six-pack stomach.

Step 2: Gather Information

Where does your client plan to work out? What type of equipment is available to him? How many days a week can he work out? For what period of time at each session? Does he travel frequently? Does he have a high-stress job? A physical job? How disciplined is your client about his diet? If dietary discipline is a problem, does he feel he can overcome it, at least temporarily? Without answering all of these questions, you will not be able to come up with specific, measurable, and realistic goals for your client.

In addition to understanding the time and equipment parameters you're working with, you need to know something about your client's current condition. Progress is a relative term, which is another way of saying that in order to see how far he's come, your client must know where he started. While I suggest that you do a thorough fitness assessment on every new client, you and your client might decide to focus on only one component of fitness, such as body fat, in which case it won't be necessary to perform all your standard tests each time you set new goals.

Step 3: Formulate Specific Goals

Walter Payton, legendary Chicago Bears running back, has often described the tremendous motivation that Bears head coach Mike Ditka provided the team by setting a specific goal. Payton said that lots of other coaches said, "We're going to play well," or, "We're going to win some games," but Ditka was the first to say, "We're going to win the Super Bowl."

The specificity of this goal, combined with a specific date and its attractiveness, was powerful. It gave the team a focus, something to hang on to when the going got tough. Armed with your data about time, equipment, and your client's current condition, as well as your gut feeling about what type of program would work for this particular client, you are ready to write specific, measurable goals and to answer the questions "What am I working so hard for?" and "How am I going to get it?"

Take a look at the sample goal map in figure 8.1. This summary is the result of a discussion with a typical, albeit hypothetical, client, a 42-year-old housewife named Connie Client. Like most women, she came to me wanting to lose weight. After measuring her body fat, we decided that a realistic goal would be for her to lose five percent body fat in four months. This was an ambitious goal, but Connie is extremely disciplined and committed, and she has enough time to work out frequently during the week. The objective of the goal map is to provide a good framework for Connie to reach her goal. First, it is very specific. Second, it tells her what she needs to do daily, weekly, and monthly. Third, it leaves no room for Connie to fool herself. This program is not a cakewalk, but if she wants to reach her body fat goal, she will need to make some sacrifices.

Step 4: Goal Conference With Your Client

I suggest that you send or give the client his copy of the goal map in advance and make plans to discuss it at your next appointment. There are several reasons to go over the map together. First, and most

---

Goal Map

Assume that on January 1, 1997, Connie Client has 28 percent body fat. She would like to reduce her body fat to 23 percent in time for the annual party at her husband's office on April 30, 1997.

Outcome Goal	**How Measured**	**Target Date**
Body fat at 23 percent	Calipers	April 30, 1997

Process Goals

Daily
Consume no more than 25 g fat
Consume no more than 1500 calories
Consume no alcohol
Consume no simple sugars

Weekly
Minimum of four cardiovascular exercise sessions, at least two at high intensity and two of longer duration
Minimum of three 40-minute resistance training sessions per week

Monthly
Two days a month eat a few extra calories (2000 maximum) as a reward
Two days a month eat a "forbidden food"—a glass of wine, candy, cookie, or similar sweet (300 calories maximum) as a reward

Reality Checks

Daily
Food diary with accurate amounts of every food, beverage, and other item consumed, including gum, supplements, cough drops—anything taken by mouth

Weekly
Weight recorded at the same time and on the same day

Monthly
Body fat measurement (calipers) and anthropometric measurements (tape)

_____ Client's initials

Figure 8.1 Sample goal map.

obvious, you want to answer any questions your client might have about the things he needs to do. Second, given the reams of paper we each receive every day, there is an unfortunate tendency to just accept that one more that we receive with a smile, only to find it weeks later crammed under the car seat. Not that you have to bring in a brass band, but the introduction of these goals and objectives should be an occasion, a notable occurrence that your client understands you take seriously and hope that he takes seriously as well. Third, you want to create some positive self-talk for your client about these goals. Focus on question 5 on his goal inventory ("When I reach this goal, here's what I will get and how I will feel") and help him create a vivid visualization of the benefits he will receive from doing all the arduous things on the goal map. For example, Connie Client responded to question 5 by saying that when she accomplished her goals she would feel "healthy, powerful, and in control." These are very empowering images that will help her focus

and give her strength on days when she is tempted to blow off her routine.

At this time, also reassure your client that you will be there to provide support and information to help stick with the process goals, by helping him figure out food labels, for example.

I suggest that you ask the client to initial the goal inventory to reinforce the importance of the goals and the understanding that you are a team committed to a common purpose.

In his remarkable book, *First Things First*, Stephen Covey writes, "Done well, traditional goal setting is powerful because it accesses the power of two of our unique endowments, creative imagination and independent will" (p.140). Encourage your client to use his creative imagination to visualize the best he can be, and support and strengthen his independent will by providing information and feedback. When you do, you will discover that goal setting is one of the most effective tools you can use to make your clients' routines productive and your work satisfying.

CHAPTER 9

Exceed Expectations Every Day: Customer Service

When I was practicing law, sometimes other lawyers would joke (at least I think they were joking), "Practicing law would be great if not for the clients!" The joke is that without clients there would be no practice of law, and therefore, no jobs for lawyers. (I can just hear all of your sympathetic sighs. No tears please!) You, too, are in a service industry, and without clients you will have no business. I've found the following rules, listed in no particular order, have served me well in giving my customers exceptional service.

**Exceed
Expectations
Every Day**

"Underpromise and overdeliver" is a motto that will never let you down.

Appreciate the Specialness of Every Client

One of the most enjoyable things about being a personal trainer is the opportunity to meet a variety of interesting, wonderful people. My clients are the greatest people in the world. I always look forward to seeing each and every one of them. They're all involved in so many different activities, and always have something interesting to say. Enjoy your clients as people. Get to know them, their interests, their dreams. Your life will be enriched and your relationships with your clients will develop into friendships. You'll be a much better motivator if you know your client as a person rather than just a collection of joints and muscles. Why is your client in your program? What motivates her to continue? In addition, you should have something to say as well. Be a well-rounded person. Be able to talk about something other than exercise if your client so desires, but be sure to remember that tact and diplomacy are always important.

Rx for Trouble

Never give a client any vitamins, supplements, tablets, pills, or other medications, including over-the-counter medications or substances (aspirin, acetaminophen, ibuprofen, analgesics, you get the idea). While these medications seem harmless, they could have seriously detrimental effects on some people. You do not know what medications this individual is currently taking or other details about her particular medical condition. Unless you are a licensed medical doctor, do not attempt to diagnose a client's medical problems. Chronic aches and pains should be reported to a physician. There are laws against unauthorized practice of medicine, which include criminal penalties. Don't break them.

Always Return Your Clients' Calls Promptly

Actively and consciously demonstrate your concern for your clients by moving them to the top of the priority list during your day, and call back immediately!

Always Be Enthusiastic About the Workout, Your Client, and Life

Yes, you have a physical job. Yes, you are tired. Still, as a coach, one of your jobs is to maintain a high degree of enthusiasm for the workout, and for life in general. Your clients are entitled to an energized motivator, not someone with the demeanor of a wrung-out dishrag.

Never Stop Learning

I'm a much better coach and motivator than I was when I began my business, and not as good as I will be by the time you read this. I know that this is true because I plan to continue attending workshops and seminars and being a voracious reader of every fitness-related publication I can get my hands on. New research comes out every day. To be the best coach and fitness professional you can be, you must be on the cutting edge of knowledge in your field. Learning and active listening go hand in hand.

Never Stop Listening

Not only do people actually enjoy finishing their sentences, you might learn something that will help you provide better service to your clients, and isn't that what you're here for? Being responsive is critical to providing excellent customer service, and you can't be responsive if you never listen!

Do What You Say You're Going to Do

Television talking heads and similar windbags, purporting to impart great insights to us little people, are incessantly waxing on the reasons that voters are "angry," or why the public is so cynical about everything. Assuming for the sake of argument that these observations are true (which I'm not saying, but go with me on this), most of us could tell them in one sentence: People get extremely annoyed when other people don't do what they say they are going to do. Is this surprising? Don't you? Be reliable.

Commit Yourself to the Continuing Pursuit of Excellence

It's amazing how much more energy and persistence you can bring to a project that you have actually committed to do. Something about making that critical choice seems to provide the strength you need when the going gets tough. I hope this book will help you begin your business with the firm determination to be your best, and that the power of that commitment will propel your level of service into the stratosphere of excellence. Be your best!

RESISTANCE WORKOUT GUIDE

CRUNCH

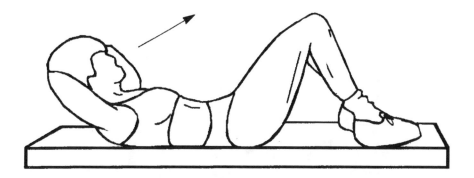

Objective: To lift the shoulders off the ground.

How to do it: Lie on your back on the floor or on a mat with your knees bent and heels close to your body. Your heels should be together; your pelvis should be tilted up and your low back pressed down to the floor or mat. Place your hands behind your head on your neck. Keeping your elbows behind your head and your chin to the ceiling, tighten your abdominals and lift your shoulders off the ground by contracting your abdominals. Continue lifting and lowering until you have completed the desired number of repetitions.

Remind your client:
- Keep your pelvis tilted up and your low back pressed firmly against the floor or mat. There should be no space between your low back and the floor. Do not arch your back.

- Keep your chin to the ceiling. Do not flex and extend your neck as you complete your repetitions. Your head should rest in a relaxed position in your hands. Your cervical vertebra should stay in a neutral, not flexed, position. If your chin is scrunched up, *stop* and readjust it so that your neck is not flexed.

- Keep your elbows behind the plane of your head. That is, do not point your elbows toward your knees.

- Emphasize the need to do this movement slowly while keeping tension on the abdominal wall.

Trainer's pointer:
- If the client finds the exercise difficult to perform with hands behind her head, suggest doing it with arms crossed across the chest. If while doing the exercise in this fashion her neck becomes tired, she should use one hand to support the neck while completing the desired number of repetitions.

TWISTING CRUNCH

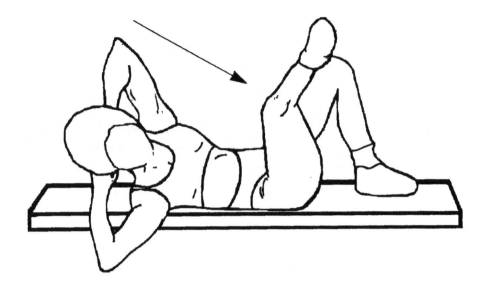

Objective: To lift the shoulder toward the opposite knee.

How to do it: Lie on your back on the floor or on a mat with your knees bent. Place your right ankle on or in the vicinity of your left knee in a cross-legged fashion. Tilt your pelvis up and press your low back into the floor. Place both hands behind your head and, keeping your pelvis flat and square on the ground, lift your left shoulder toward your right knee. Repeat for the desired number of repetitions, then switch legs and shoulders.

Remind your client:
- Do the exercise in a controlled fashion.
- Keep your pelvis flat and square on the floor. The twisting should come at the waist.
- Do not twist or pull on your neck during the exercise. Your chin should stay in line with the center of your body at all times.
- Do not arch your back.
- Keep your neck relaxed. If it is flexed so that you have a double chin, *stop* and readjust.

Trainer's pointer:
- Your client must keep her pelvis flat and in contact with the floor. The rotation should occur at her waist.

OBLIQUE CRUNCH

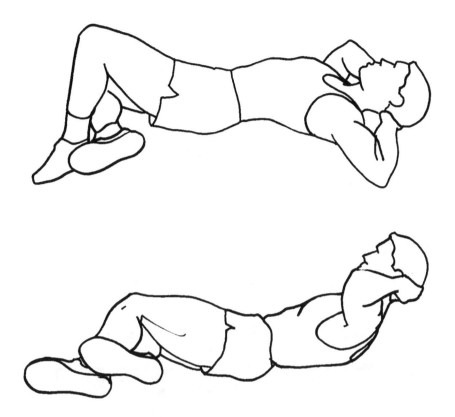

Objective: To lift the shoulder off the ground.

How to do it: Lie on your back. Place your hands behind your head. Bring your knees together and drop them to one side. Lift your shoulders toward your hips as if you were doing a crunch. After completing the desired number of repetitions, repeat with knees on the other side.

Remind your client: • Activate your transverse abdominis, the deepest abdominal muscle by trying to pull your iliac crests (the two hip bones just below and to each side of your navel) together so they meet under your navel.

                          • Do not pull on your neck.

Trainer's pointers: • Do not allow your client to pull on his neck. Tell him to imagine that he has a cantaloupe between his chin and chest, and to keep his chin toward the ceiling. Also, suggest that he keep his elbows behind his head, which will also reduce the risk of neck pulling. If he has difficulty keeping his neck relaxed, try having him place each hand on the top of the opposite shoulder blade and rest his head in his crossed arms.

                          • Check activation of the transverse abdominis before and during the exercise.

                          • This is an advanced exercise that requires back and hip flexibility.

LYING LEG RAISE

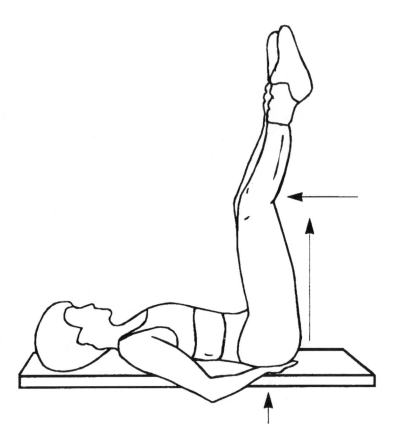

Objective: To flex the spine and lift the pelvis toward the rib cage.

How to do it: Lie on your back on the floor or on a mat. Tilt your pelvis up and place your hands under your glutes like a wedge to tilt your pelvis and support your lower back. Keeping your knees straight (your knees can be soft but not actively bent), try to touch the ceiling with your pointed toes. Concentrate on flexing your pelvis and lifting your gluteus using your lower abdominals.

Remind your client: • Do not arch your back.

• Keep your pelvis tilted up.

• Keep your shoulders relaxed.

• Keep your wrists flat on the floor or mat.

• Do not flex and extend knees.

Trainer's pointers: • Suggest that your client think of this exercise as a pelvic tilt, the only difference being that the legs are off the ground.

• Tell your client to keep her transverse abdominis tight, and reinforce this during the exercise.

REVERSE CRUNCH

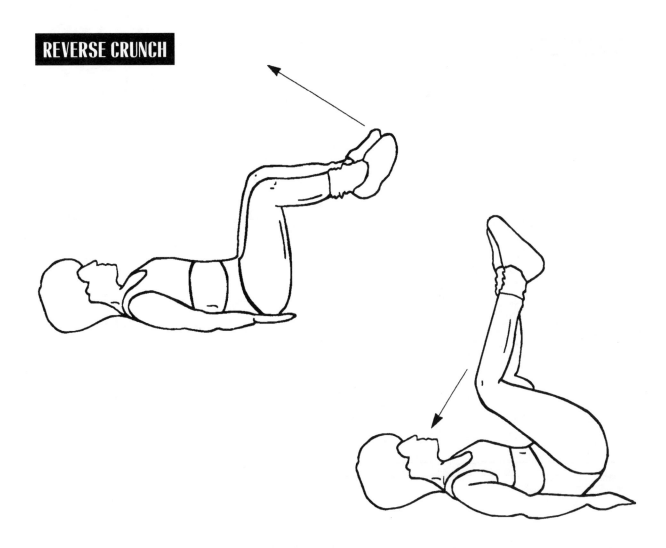

Objective:	To move the pelvis toward the rib cage.
How to do it:	Lie on your back with your feet on the floor and your knees flexed 90 degrees. Place your hands under your glutes so that they can act as a wedge to tilt the pelvis up. Keeping the knees at 90 degrees of flexion, lift your hips off the floor.
Remind your client:	• Feel each vertebra lifting off the floor.
	• Don't move the thighs back and forth; the objective is to lift the pelvis, not the legs.
	• Keep the shoulders and neck relaxed.
	• Keep the transverse abdominis tight.
	• Lower the pelvis very slowly.
Trainer's pointers:	• A useful cue: Tell your client that this movement is exactly like a pelvic tilt, except the feet are off the ground.
	• Watch for the tendency to move the thighs rather than the pelvis. Emphasize the need to keep the knees flexed at 90 degrees throughout the range of motion.

SINGLE HIP FLEXION

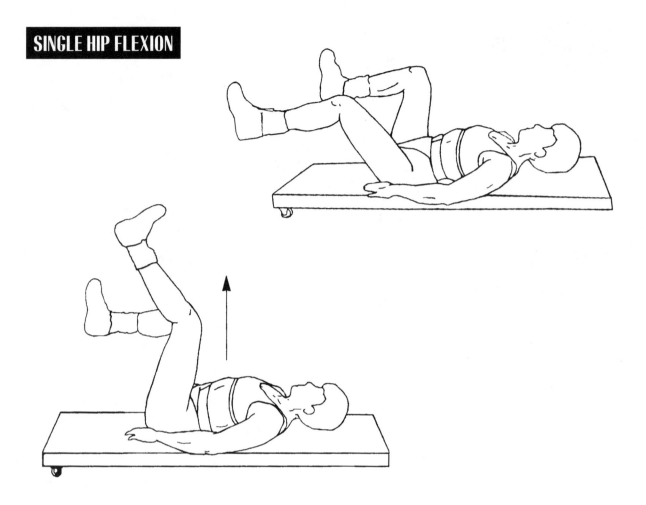

Objective: To lift and lower the leg by flexing the hip.

How to do it: Lie on your back. Lift your feet off the floor and flex your knees to 90 degrees. Keep the natural curve in your low back. Don't press the low back down or tilt the pelvis. Tighten the transverse abdominis. Straighten the left leg to approximately 45 degrees of flexion. Keeping the left knee frozen, move the left leg toward the floor until the heel almost but doesn't quite touch the floor or mat. Return to the start position. Repeat for the required number of repetitions. Re-adjust the transverse abdominis muscle by tightening it, then perform the same number of repetitions on the other side.

Remind your client:
- Keep your transverse abdominis tight.
- Keep the knee frozen. The axis of rotation is the hip.

Trainer's pointers:
- This exercise works on the muscles in the low back that stabilize the pelvis.
- Before your client begins the exercise, check the activation of the transverse abdominis by placing your finger on his lower abdominals. It is critical that he maintain this activation throughout the exercise.
- Be sure your client maintains the natural curve in his back. He should not press his low back down.
- Beginners should do this exercise with the knee of the working leg flexed 90 degrees. The straighter the leg, the more difficult the exercise.

BICYCLE CRUNCH

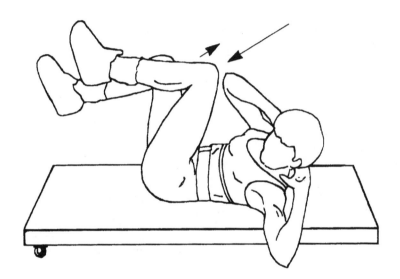

Objective:	To lift and rotate the shoulder and the opposite thigh by flexing the spine.
How to do it:	Lie on your back with the knees bent. Place the hands behind the head. Lift the feet off the floor. Tilt the pelvis up and press the low back down. Begin with the knees at 90 degrees of flexion and the elbows behind the ears. Lift and twist the right shoulder while bringing the left knee in to meet it. Repeat for the required number of repetitions. Switch sides.
Remind your client:	• Don't rotate or flex the neck.
	• Keep the elbows back behind the head.
	• Focus on rotating the spine. Visualize the flat, trim waist you're working for.
	• Keep the transverse abdominis activated.
Trainer's pointer:	• Neck rotation is a real problem on this one. Suggest that your client try to keep his chin in line with his sternum.

STRAIGHT LEG U-CRUNCH

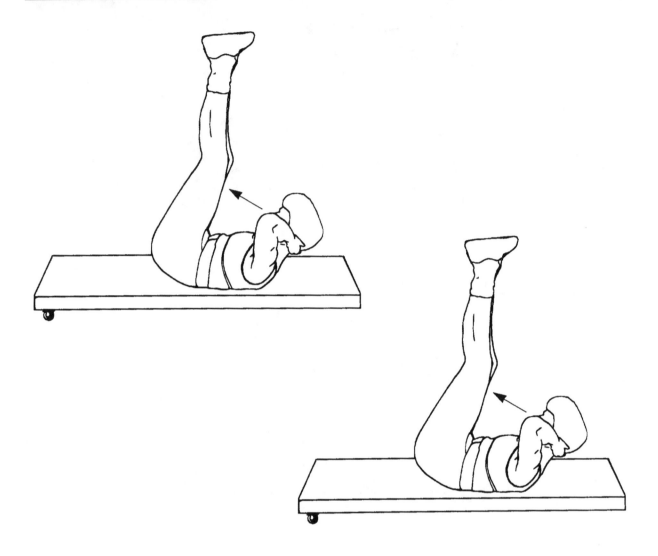

Objective:	To lift and rotate the pelvis toward the rib cage while lifting the shoulders off the ground.
How to do it:	Lie on your back. Place your hands behind your head. Lift the feet off the floor and straighten the legs so that the heels are facing the ceiling. Tighten the transverse abdominis. Keeping the knees rigid, lift the pelvis toward the ceiling.
Remind your client:	• Relax the neck and shoulders.
	• Do the exercise slowly and under control. Don't bounce your low back off the floor (ouch!).
	• Keep the elbows back behind the ears.
Trainer's pointers:	• Encourage your client to think of lifting the pelvis and rotating it toward the rib cage, not just lifting the legs up and down. Suggest that she focus on feeling each vertebra returning to the floor as the pelvis lowers on each repetition.
	• Watch for flexion and extension at the knees. They should stay frozen.

BENT KNEE U-CRUNCH

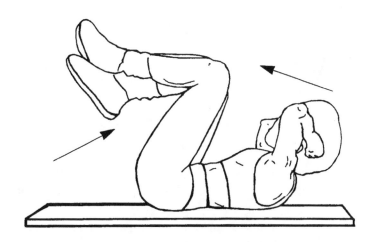

Objective:	To lift the pelvis and rib cage toward each other.
How to do it:	Lie on your back. Flex your knees to 90 degrees and lift your feet off the ground. Place your hands behind your head. Simultaneously lift your shoulders and pelvis toward each other. Return to start position.
Remind your client:	• Keep your neck relaxed.
	• Do not bounce your pelvis off the ground. This should be a controlled lift.
	• Keep the transverse abdominis activated.
Trainer's pointers:	• Do not allow your client to pull on her neck. Tell her to imagine she has a cantaloupe between her chin and chest, and to keep her chin toward the ceiling. Also suggest that she keep her elbows back behind her head, which will reduce the risk of neck pulling.
	• Make sure your client squeezes and tightens her abdominals at the top of the movement.

HANGING LEG RAISE

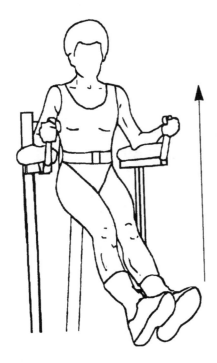
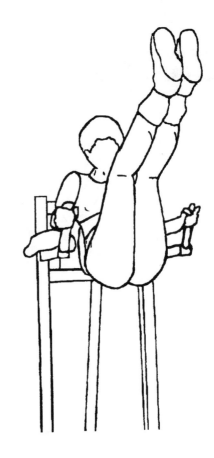

Objective: To lift and rotate the pelvis toward the rib cage.

How to do it: This exercise has three variations:

1. Hang from a chin-up bar by holding on with your hands.

2. Hang from a chin-up bar while supported under your upper arms using specially designed straps.

3. Rest your elbows and forearms on the pads of a specially designed elevated chair found in many gyms and clubs.

Begin with the legs straight, or with the knees only slightly bent. Keep your knees rigid and lift your legs until your thighs are at a 90 degree angle to your torso. Continue curling your lower body by lifting your pelvis up toward your rib cage. Actively contract your abdominal muscles. Return to the start position and repeat for the required number of repetitions.

Remind your client:
- Don't do the exercise ballistically by swinging your legs up and down. Instead, focus on lifting the pelvis.

- Squeeze the abdominals. Feel the active contraction.

Trainer's pointers:
- This is an advanced exercise. Your client should not attempt it until she finds lying leg raises and U-crunches no longer challenging. In addition, clients who have excessive body fat shouldn't attempt this exercise because the excess weight will put too much stress on the elbows and wrists.

- If your client cannot perform this exercise with good form, but you think she is ready for something beyond lying leg raises, try the bent knee version.

- Sometimes you see people using ankle weights while doing this exercise. This is not recommended due to the risk of excess stress on the ankles.

HANGING KNEE RAISE

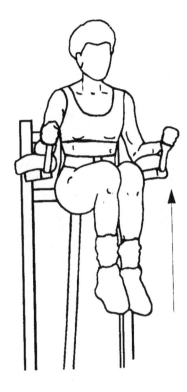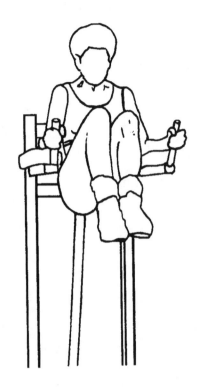

Objective:	To lift and rotate the pelvis.
How to do it:	The three position variations for the hanging leg raise can be applied here, too (see p. 76). Begin with the knees bent at 90 degrees of flexion. Keep your knees rigid and lift your legs and pelvis up toward your rib cage. Actively contract your abdominal muscles. Return to start position and repeat for the required number of repetitions.
Remind your client:	• Keep the knees rigid. Focus on moving the pelvis.
	• Actively contract the abdominals on each repetition.
	• Don't swing the legs up and down. Move slowly and under control.
Trainer's pointer:	• It should be possible to lift the pelvis much higher in this exercise than in the hanging leg raise. Take advantage of this to help your client achieve a more powerful contraction.

LAT PULLDOWN

Objective: To pull the resistance down by squeezing the shoulder blades back and down.

How to do it: Grasp the bar at a universal or other pulldown machine. Sit down. Let your latissimus dorsi (lats) stretch out. Pull the bar down to your sternum while simultaneously arching your back and sticking out your chest. Lean back at about a 70 degree angle. Pull the stack down in the following sequence: pull shoulder blades toward spine, flex elbows, depress shoulder blades (that is, pull the shoulder blades down and back).

Remind your client:
- Do not hunch forward as you pull down. The shoulder should retract before the elbow flexes. Think of it like this: "Shoulder comes in, elbow comes in, chest goes out."
- Do not "turtle," that is, shrug your shoulder blades up toward your ears; your trapezius should be relaxed.

Trainer's pointers:
- Make sure your client pulls her scapula back ("retract") and then down ("depress"). Use the tactile cue described in "Pulldown Behind the Head" (p. 80).
- Make sure your client's torso does not move back and forth in a rocking motion. Keep the abdominals tight and maintain the four-finger space between the pelvis and rib cage.
- If your client hunches forward as she pulls down, reduce the weight.

CLOSE-GRIP PULLDOWN

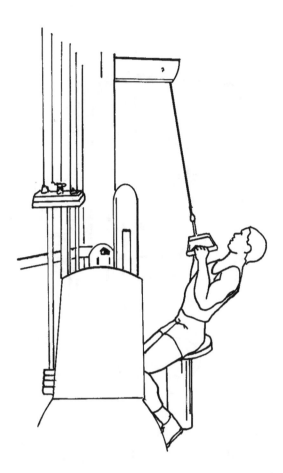

Objective:	To pull the handle to your rib cage.
How to do it:	Grasp the close-grip handle attached to the cable of a lat pulldown machine. Sit down on the seat. Lean back and allow your lats to stretch out. Pull the stack down in the following sequence: pull shoulder blades toward spine, flex elbows, depress shoulder blades (that is, pull the shoulder blades down and back). Try to get your elbows back as far as possible.
Remind your client:	• Don't turtle.
	• Don't hunch forward.
	• Don't rock the body.
	• Keep the arms close to the body.
Trainer's pointers:	• During the exercise, place your hands on top of the client's shoulders. If you feel clicking and popping, suggest that he depress his scapula and relax his neck.
	• Watch for wrist flexion and extension. Your client's wrists should stay straight.

PULLDOWN BEHIND THE HEAD

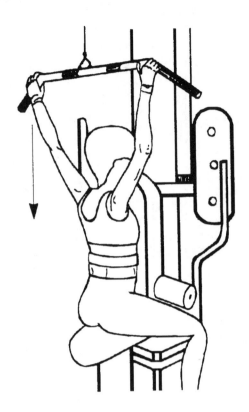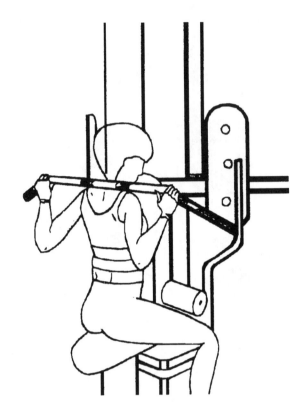

Objective: To pull the resistance down by squeezing the shoulder blades together.

How to do it: Grasp the bar at a universal or pulldown machine. Sit down. Let your lats stretch out. Pull the bar down behind your head until it touches the base of your neck by pulling the shoulder blades back, flexing the elbows, then depressing the shoulder blades.

Remind your client:
- Make sure you pull your shoulder blades in and down *before* your elbows flex. Don't hunch forward as you pull down. Do not shrug your shoulders up toward your ears. Try to keep your upper trapezius relaxed while activating the lower trapezius. Think of it as "retract scapula, flex elbows, depress scapula."

- Do not bend forward at the waist.

Trainer's pointers:
- Try to keep your client's upper trapezius relaxed while she activates the lower trapezius. I find it useful to put my fingers just below the inferior angle of the scapula and have the client activate the lower trapezius to get a feel for it so she'll know what to focus on when she pulls her scapula down.

- **Caution:** Because of the extreme external shoulder rotation in this exercise, it is inappropriate for people with rotator cuff problems. Some authorities believe it should be eliminated from all programs because of the risk of injury. When in doubt, substitute the lat pulldown.

- Place your hand at the back of the client's head to prevent her from whacking herself on every rep.

SEATED ROW

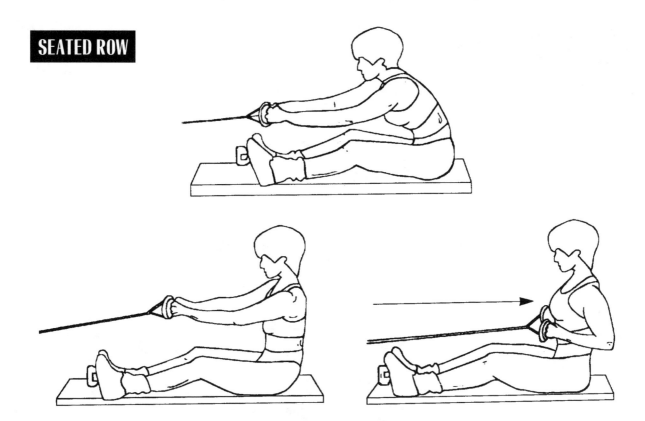

Objective: To pull the resistance by squeezing the shoulder blades in toward the spine.

How to do it: Sit facing the low pulley of a machine with either a short straight bar handle or a close-grip handle. Grasp the handle and position your body so that your knees are slightly bent (about 150 degrees). You should be leaning forward in a beginning rowing position. Row the handle by straightening your body, pulling your shoulder blades in, and, finally, flexing your elbow, in that order. Squeeze your shoulder blades and stick your chest out in a military position and return to the starting position.

Remind your client:
- Keep your back flat and your head up during the exercise.
- Do not flex your elbows until your shoulder blades have retracted into your spine.
- Remember to do the exercise under control, especially during the negative (return) portion of the exercise.
- Do not allow the stack to jerk your elbows into an extended position.
- Don't turtle—keep your upper trapezius relaxed.
- Don't flex and extend your knees. They should remain motionless.
- To achieve the right "military posture" in the last movement of the exercise, imagine a cadet standing at attention.
- Create and maintain the four-finger space between your pelvis and rib cage. Keep your back flat.

Trainer's pointers:
- Make sure your client is not only retracting, but also depressing her scapula during this exercise.
- Watch for flexion or extension at the wrists and knees or spinal rotation.
- Watch the position of your client's elbows. They should stay close to the body. If they flare out, your client is probably "turtleing."

INCLINE DUMBBELL ROW

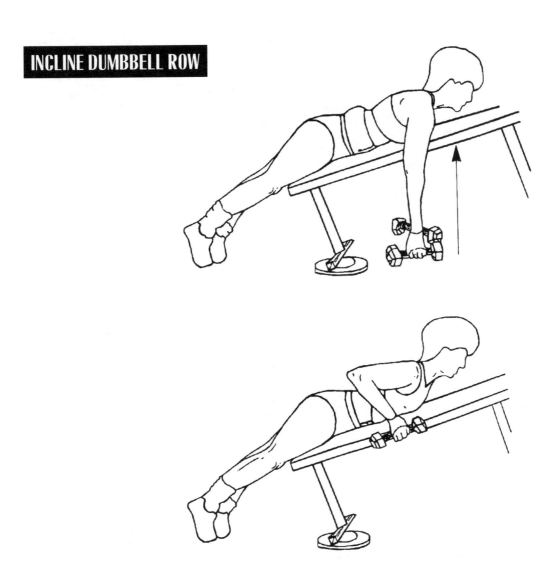

Objective:	To lift the resistance by pulling the shoulder blades back and down.
How to do it:	Lie on your stomach on an incline bench or other elevated bench. Grasp a dumbbell in each hand. Reach out toward the ground. (You should feel a stretch in your lats.) The dumbbells should be at about a 45 degree angle to the bench. Pull your shoulder blades in toward your spine, then flex your elbows. Squeeze your shoulder blades together and arch your back.
Remind your client:	• Make sure that you pull your shoulder blades in before you flex your elbows.
	• Do not flex or extend your knees.
	• Keep your neck straight and your back flat.
Trainer's pointers:	• Watch your client's spine and make sure it doesn't twist.
	• Make sure your client does not round her back.
	• Make sure the weight is not so heavy that your client cannot hold it straight. If you notice that she holds the dumbbell so it is hanging off her hand with one end lower than the other, this means that her wrist flexors and extensors can't handle this much resistance. Reduce the weight to avoid elbow tendinitis.
	• I suggest that you place the bench against a wall for safety.

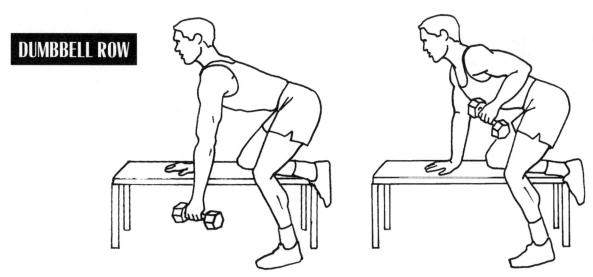

DUMBBELL ROW

Objective:	To lift the resistance by pulling the shoulder blade in toward the spine.
How to do it:	Grasp a dumbbell in one hand. Stand next to a flat bench, lean forward, and place the opposite hand on the bench. Place the knee on the side of the resting hand on the bench to support your back. At this point, your torso should be parallel with the ground. Lift the dumbbell up by first pulling your shoulder blade and flexing your elbow. Your elbow should be very close to your side at hip level at the top of your movement. Squeeze your shoulder blades together.
Remind your client:	• Concentrate on pulling your shoulder blades in toward your spine and down toward your low back.
	• Don't turtle.
	• Don't swing the dumbbell.
	• Keep your wrists straight. Do not allow them to flex or extend.
	• Keep the knee of the supporting leg slightly bent, but rigid. Do not flex and extend the supporting leg to provide additional momentum in the exercise.
	• Your weight should be resting on the supporting leg, not on the supporting wrist.
	• Keep your back flat, not rounded. Keep abdominals tight to stabilize the spine.
	• Do not twist your torso.
	• Create and maintain the four-finger space between your pelvis and rib cage.
	• Keep the neck straight to keep the cervical vertebra (vertebra in the neck) in a neutral position.
Trainer's pointers:	• Keep your eye on your client's scapula. Make sure he's pulling it down and back, not up toward the ears. Make sure the scapula of the supporting side is in line with his spinal column.
	• Make sure your client doesn't flex and extend his supporting knee.
	• If your client can't keep the dumbbell straight in his hand, that is, if one end hangs down toward the ground, it's too heavy for his forearms. Reduce the weight.
	• If your client has a hard time keeping his back flat, try doing this on an incline bench (supporting hand on incline portion, supporting leg on seat).
	• Watch for spinal rotation, especially during the last few reps.
	• Make sure the working arm stays close to the body. Excessive upper arm abduction can put undesirable stress on the shoulder.
	• Make sure the client's weight is on his supporting leg, not supporting wrist.

DUMBBELL PULLOVER

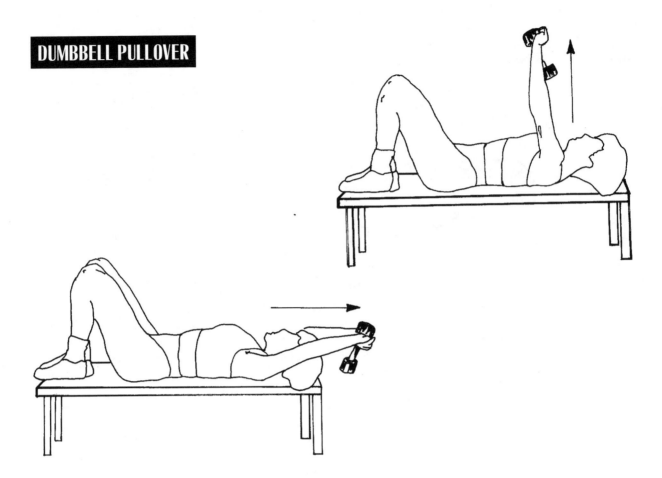

Objective:

To move the upper arms parallel with the head.

How to do it:

Lie on your back on a flat bench with your knees bent and your feet flat up on the bench. Hold one dumbbell with both hands around the plate portion at one end. Begin with your arms extended, elbows slightly bent and facing out (shoulders externally rotated), and the dumbbell at the level of your sternum. Move the dumbbell by lowering your upper arms toward your head. When the dumbbell is at the same level as the bench and slightly behind your head, return it to the starting position.

Remind your client:

- The axis of rotation is your shoulder joint. Keep your elbows slightly bent, but do not flex and extend them during the exercise. They should be rigid.

- Do not take the dumbbell farther back behind your head than the point at which you can bring it forward under full control. You should never lower the dumbbell past the point at which your arms are parallel with your ears.

- Your head, back, gluteus, and feet should always remain in contact with the bench.

- Do not arch your back.

- Do not flex and extend your wrists.

Trainer's pointers:

- If you begin this exercise by handing the dumbbell to your client, do not let go of it until she tells you she has it.

- Spot your client by placing your hand near the bottom part of the dumbbell.

- Ask your client if there is any clicking or popping in her shoulders. Place your hands there and feel for unwanted snap, crackle, or pop.

- Watch for the tendency to rotate internally at the shoulder. The elbows should point out throughout the movement.

CHIN-UP

Objective:	To lift the body with the arms and back.
How to do it:	Place a sturdy chair or bench in front of a chin-up bar. Step up on it and grasp the bar. Your grip should be slightly wider than shoulder width. Lift your feet off the bench. Keeping your head back, lift your body toward the bar. Try to touch your chest to the bar. Arch your back and feel for a peak contraction in the lats.
Remind your client:	• Don't hunch forward. Keep the head up.
	• Focus on the motion of the scapula, which should be back and down.
	• Arch your back into exaggerated military posture at the peak of the movement. Feel your shoulder blades squeeze together.
Trainer's pointers:	• Obviously, this is an advanced exercise and as such, should not be done by unconditioned individuals, especially those who are overweight. Establish a good base of conditioning before it is attempted. Failure to follow this advice is sure to result in elbow and shoulder problems.
	• Form is extremely important on chin-ups to keep the targeted muscles working.
	• Some commentators suggest that it is safer to use a palms-facing grip (with the palms facing each other) to avoid the risk of injury from excessive external shoulder rotation.

PREACHER CURL

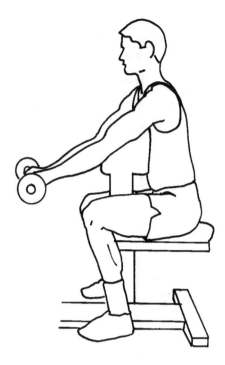 

Objective:	To flex the elbows.
How to do it:	Sit on a preacher bench. It should be adjusted so that the armpits rest on the top part of the bench and the feet are flat on the floor with the knees at 90 degrees of flexion. Lean forward and grab the bar, which may be angled or straight. Position yourself with hands shoulder-width apart and your armpits resting against the bench. The top of the bench should hit you at about collarbone level. Curl the bar up to your chin and lower the weight to repeat. Keep your wrists straight during the exercise.
Remind your client:	• Keep your shoulders and chest against the bench during the exercise. Move only at the elbow joints.
Trainer's pointer:	• Make sure your client goes through a full range of motion by straightening (but not hyperextending) his elbows on each repetition.

BARBELL CURL

Objective:	To flex the elbows.
How to do it:	Grasp a straight or angled bar with a shoulder-width (or slightly wider), palms-up grip. Position yourself so that your feet are firmly planted and your knees are slightly bent. Keeping your upper arms against the sides of your body, curl the bar up by flexing at the elbow joint.
Remind your client:	• Keep your body still. Do not rock your back.
	• Your wrists should remain straight during the exercise. There is no need to flex your wrists at the top of the movement.
	• Remember to lower the bar to a count of four while raising it to a count of two.
Trainer's pointers:	• If your client has trouble keeping her back from rocking, make sure she keeps her knees soft. If that fails, have her do this exercise standing against a wall and reduce the weight.
	• Suggest that your client lock her elbows against her rib cage.

SEATED DUMBBELL CURL

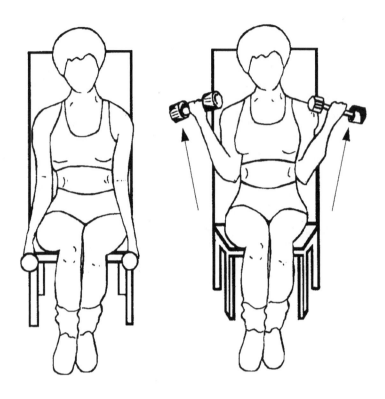

Objective: To flex the elbow and turn the hand.

How to do it: Sit on a bench with a back support. Grasp a dumbbell in each hand, palms facing your sides. Curl the weight up by flexing at the elbow. Simultaneously rotate your forearm. At the peak of the movement, your palm should be facing up with the little finger higher than the thumb.

Remind your client: • Make sure your upper arm stays next to and slightly in front of the center of your upper body. Do not let the elbow move away from the body, because this takes the tension off the biceps and stresses the elbow.

• This exercise can be done one arm at a time or both arms at the same time.

Trainer's pointer: • As your client fatigues, watch for the tendency for the upper arms to move forward. If necessary to keep the upper arms still and against the body, stand behind the client and hold them in place.

CONCENTRATION CURL

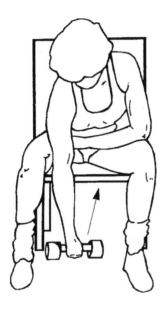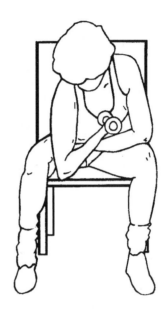

Objective: To flex the elbow and turn the hand so that the little finger is higher than the thumb.

How to do it: Sit on a bench and grasp a dumbbell in one hand. Your knees should be apart, feet flat on the floor. Lean forward and place the forearm and elbow of the working arm (the one grasping the dumbbell) against the thigh on the same side of the body with the palm facing you. Curl the weight up by flexing at the elbow joint. As you flex your elbow, turn forearm so that at the top of the movement your palm is up. Squeeze the biceps at the top of the movement and lower the weight to the starting position.

Remind your client: • Keep your upper arm firmly planted against your thigh. Do not rock your body during the exercise.

Trainer's pointers: • Watch your client's shoulder on the side of the working arm. It should be relaxed.

• Make sure your client keeps her wrist straight while performing the exercise.

STANDING CALF RAISE

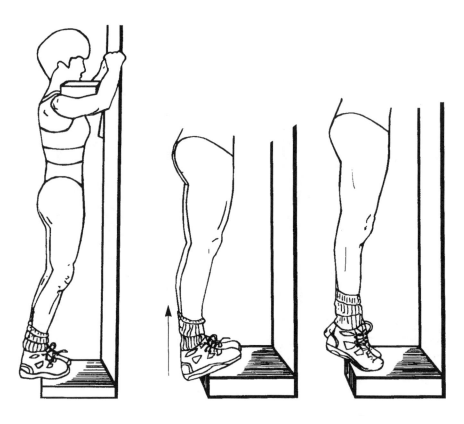

Objective:	To flex and point the toes.
How to do it:	Stand at the calf raise station of the universal machine or hold a dumbbell in your hand for resistance. If you are using a machine, crouch down under the pad and raise it by standing up straight. If you are doing the exercise with a dumbbell, stand on a bottom stair or a stable bench (maximum height of six inches) with your heels off the edge. Keeping your knees locked (but not hyperextended), raise up and down on your toes.
Remind your client:	• Keep your knees locked but not hyperextended.
	• Drop your heels in a slow, controlled manner as low as possible on the way down and come up as high as possible at the top. Hold the peak contraction for a second when you are up on your toes.
Trainer's pointers:	• Make sure your client goes through a full range of motion. There is a tendency to stop descending before the heels have dropped to their maximum depth.
	• Try varying foot positions (parallel, toes in, and toes out) to work all angles of the gastrocnemius.

SEATED CALF RAISE

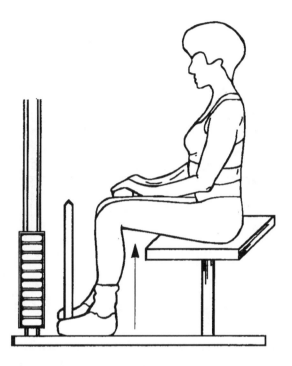 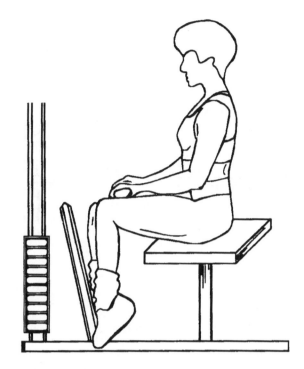

Objective:	To flex and point the toes.
How to do it:	Sit at a seated calf raise machine. Place your knees under the pad after adjusting it so that your knee is at a 90 degree angle while you are seated. With your feet firmly on the platform, release the stack and allow your heel to drop to its lowest range of motion. Press the stack up by flexing at the ankle joint.
Remind your client:	• Do the exercise slowly and under control. Your upper body should be relaxed. No bouncing, twisting, or similar histrionics (yes, it's supposed to really burn).
Trainer's pointers:	• Your client should keep her upper body relaxed. • Watch ROM as in the standing calf raise.

BENCH PRESS

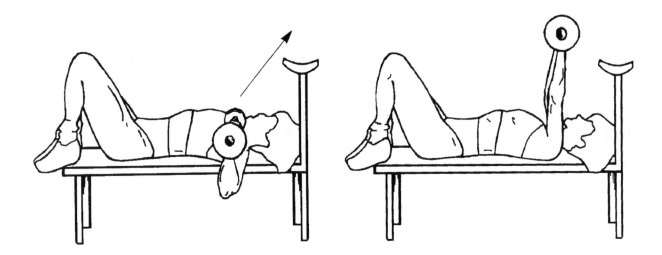

Objective:	To straighten the arms and bring them toward the center of the body by squeezing the pectorals together.
How to do it:	Lie on your back on a flat bench with your feet up on the bench. Grasp the bar with your hands slightly wider than shoulder width, palms facing forward, elbows bent. Your elbows, shoulders, and wrists should stay in the same plane during the exercise. Press the bar straight up by straightening, but not hyperextending your arms. Breathe out as you raise the bar. The bar should travel in a slightly diagonal line, that is, the angle formed by your upper arms and your upper body should be approximately 78 degrees, not 90 degrees.

Remind your client:

- Control your wrists. They should stay straight and rigid and should not flex or extend.

- Do not bounce the bar off your chest.

- Your head, back, and glutes should stay in contact with the bench at all times. Do not arch your back!

- Keep elbows in line with shoulders.

- It is *strongly* recommended that you have a spotter when you do the bench press.

Trainer's pointers:

- Remind your client to inhale while lowering the bar and exhale while raising it. Don't allow your client to hold her breath, as this causes serious increases in blood pressure.

- The bar should not touch your client's chest when she lowers it. Stop her just short of chest level.

- If the bench is too short for your client to comfortably put her feet up on it, place another bench at the end for this purpose.

INCLINE DUMBBELL PRESS

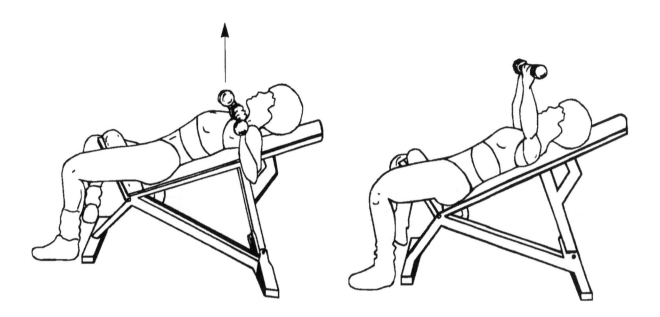

Objective:	To straighten the arms and bring them toward the center of the body.
How to do it:	Lie on your back on an incline bench. Grasp one dumbbell in each hand, with palms facing forward, elbows bent, dumbbells just to the sides of your shoulders. Your elbows and shoulders should be in a straight line. Press the dumbbells straight up by straightening, but not hyperextending your arms at the elbow. The dumbbells should travel in a diagonal line so that when your arms are straight the ends of the dumbbells are together. Focus on squeezing your pectorals at the top of the movement.
Remind your client:	• Make sure your back is flat on the bench. Your knees should be bent and your feet should be flat on the floor to keep you from arching your back.
	• Do not allow your wrists to flex or extend.
	• Remember that the advantage of using dumbbells is that you are able to lower them deeper than you would be able to lower a bar and feel a better stretch in your pectorals before you begin to press the dumbbells up.
	• Control the position of your forearms. Do not allow your shoulders to rotate out of the proper plane. Your wrists should stay in the same plane with your elbows and shoulders.
Trainer's pointers:	• If your client seems to have trouble keeping her back down on the bench, have her put her feet on a flat bench placed at the end of the incline bench.
	• If you notice that your client can't keep her elbows and wrists in the same plane with her shoulders, reduce the weight.

FLAT DUMBBELL PRESS

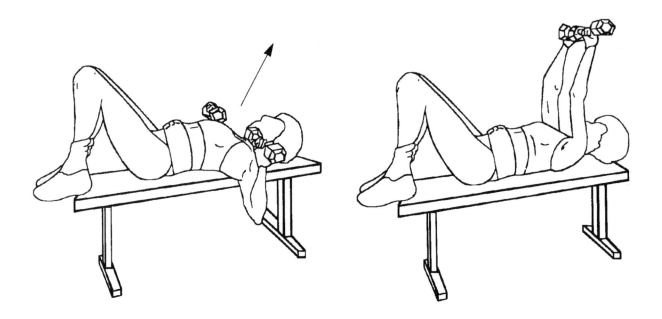

Objective:	To straighten the arms and bring them toward the center of the body by squeezing the pectorals together.
How to do it:	Lie on your back on a flat bench with your feet up on the bench. Grasp one dumbbell in each hand, with palms facing forward, elbows bent, dumbbells just to the side of your shoulders. Your elbows, shoulders, and wrists should be in the same plane. Your knuckles should face the ceiling. Press the dumbbells up by straightening, but not hyperextending your arms. At the top of the movement, the dumbbells should be over your chin.
Remind your client:	• Don't let your wrists flop around. Keep them straight.
	• Control the dumbbells so that they are close to your body. When your elbows are bent, the inner part of the dumbbells should touch your shoulders.
	• Control the position of your forearms. Remember to keep elbows and shoulders in the same plane.
Trainer's pointer:	• Watch the position of your client's forearms. If you notice that they are moving toward her pelvis so that the dumbbells are below nipple level when she lowers them, this means that her rotator cuffs can't control the resistance. Reduce the weight and review proper form.

BARBELL INCLINE PRESS

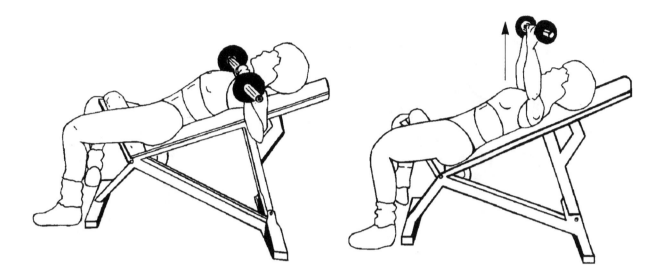

Objective:	To press the bar upward by straightening the arms.
How to do it:	Lie on your back on an incline bench. Grasp a bar with an evenly spaced grip approximately six inches wider than shoulder width. Have your trainer or spotter help you unrack the bar. Keeping your elbows in line with your shoulders, slowly lower the bar to within one inch of your chest and press it back up by straightening, but not hyperextending the arms.
Remind your client:	• Keep your back flat and completely on the bench.
	• Control your wrists. They should stay straight.
	• Do not bounce the bar off your chest.
	• Go through a full range of motion. Be sure to extend at the shoulder joint, not just flex the elbow.
Trainer's pointers:	• Watch your client's back. Make sure it stays in contact with the bench. Some clients need to put their feet up on another bench to make sure the back stays flat.
	• Watch the relative position of elbows and shoulders. Make sure your client keeps them in line and doesn't allow her upper body to droop toward the lower body.

 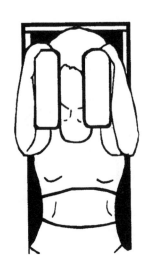

Objective:	To squeeze the elbows together.
How to do it:	Sit on the chair of a pec deck machine or the pec deck attachment of a universal machine. Adjust the seat so that your elbows are at a 90 degree angle when your arms are on the pads. Place your forearms on the pads and bring the pads together by contracting your pectorals. Squeeze your pectorals at the peak of contraction. After the set is completed, release one pad at a time by turning your torso in the direction of the pad.
Remind your client:	• Be *absolutely certain* that you have the weight stack under control. This exercise is one in which you should be extremely cautious about using excessive weight, since your arm is in a position of abduction and external rotation, the most vulnerable position for your rotator cuff. It is essential that you do not lose control of the weight stack. Therefore, be sure not to allow your arms to move outside the same plane as your head.
	• Push through with your forearms, not with your hands. Think of trying to bring your elbows together.
	• Keep your upper body relaxed. You should move only at the shoulder joint.
	• Don't turtle. Your upper trapezius should be relaxed.
Trainer's pointers:	• **Caution:** The beginning position, shoulder abduction and external rotation, is one of the most vulnerable positions for the rotator cuff. Be careful!
	• Make sure your client does not allow her upper arms to go behind the plane her head is in. Avoid excessive external shoulder rotation.
	• Make sure your client doesn't rock her body.
	• Spot your client by making sure she doesn't exceed a controllable range of motion.

FLYS

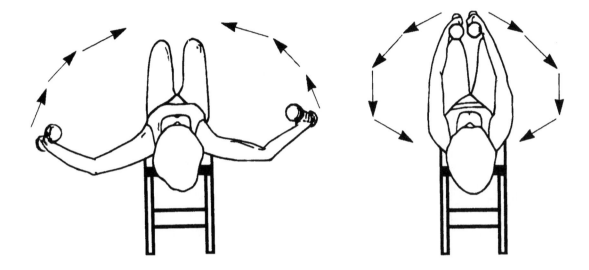

Objective: To move the upper arms in toward the center of the body.

How to do it: Lie on your back on a flat or incline bench. Grasp one dumbbell in each hand. Begin the exercise by positioning your arms so that they extend overhead with your elbows slightly bent and the dumbbells in a palms-together position, touching. I sometimes call this exercise the "barrel squeeze" because the idea is to squeeze the dumbbells together as if you were squeezing a barrel. Slowly, and under control, lower your upper arms until they are in line and parallel with the bench (no lower) and return them to the starting position by squeezing your pectorals.

Remind your client:
- Keep your upper body relaxed. You should move only at the shoulder joint.
- Keep your back down on the bench. If you are doing the exercise on an incline bench your feet should be flat on the floor with your knees flexed. If you are doing the exercise on a flat bench, your knees should be bent and your feet should be up on the bench.
- Keep your elbows, wrists, and shoulders in the same plane at all times.
- Make sure to keep your elbow joints rigid. It is a common mistake to flex elbow joints during the exercise, which turns it into a press rather than a fly. If you feel the need to do this, reduce the amount of weight you're using.

Trainer's pointers:
- Don't let your client lower her upper arms below the bench.
- Don't let your client flex and extend her elbows when she lowers the weights. If she can't keep her elbows rigid, reduce the weight and work up to something heavier.
- Warn your client of the risk of banging her fingers.
- If your client is doing this exercise on an incline bench and cannot keep her feet on the floor while keeping the knees bent, place another bench at her feet to use as a footrest.

REVERSE BARBELL CURL

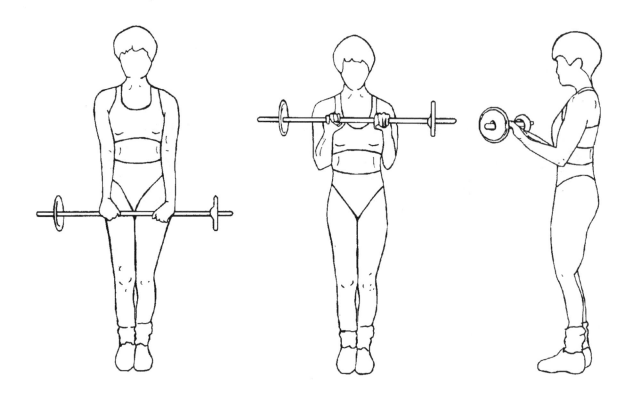

Objective:	To lift the barbell by flexing the arm at the elbow.
How to do it:	Stand and hold a bar in front of you. You should have a palms-down grip with your hands approximately shoulder-width apart. Keeping your upper arms against your body, curl the bar up and toward your body. Repeat for the required number of repetitions.
Remind your client:	• Keep the wrists rigid. Don't flex and extend at the wrist.
	• Don't rock your body. No spinal extension, please!
	• Keep the neck relaxed.
	• Keep your upper arms firmly against your body.
Trainer's pointers:	• If your client flexes and extends her wrists, elbow tendinitis is a distinct possibility. Watch for this.
	• Discourage excessive gripping. Yes, she needs to hold on to the bar. But she doesn't need to grip it as tightly as if she were hanging from a 500-foot drop.
	• Be sure your client maintains her four-finger space between the pelvis and rib cage.

REVERSE DUMBBELL CURL

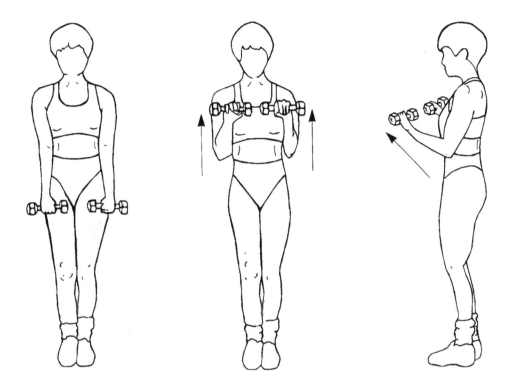

Objective: To lift dumbbells by flexing the arms at the elbows.

How to do it: This exercise is identical to the barbell curl except that, instead of a palms-up (supinated) grip, you grasp the dumbbells with your palms down (pronated). Keep your upper arms firmly against your body and raise the weight by flexing at the elbow joint.

Remind your client: • Do not rock your body during the exercise. The only action should be at the elbow joint. If you need to rock your body back and forth, reduce the amount of weight. Keep your knees soft and relaxed.

Trainer's pointer: • Make sure your client keeps her knees soft and relaxed, which will help her keep her body from rocking. If she rocks her body even when her knees are relaxed, have her do the exercise with her back against the wall.

WRIST FLEXION

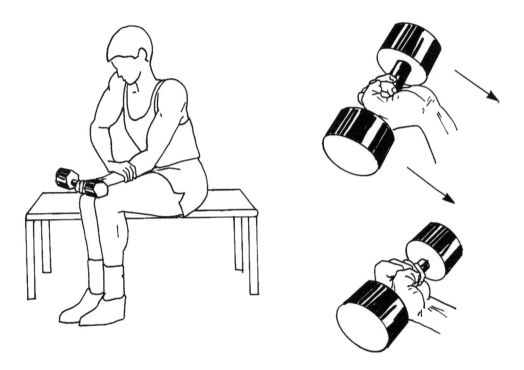

Objective: To flex the wrist.

How to do it: This exercise can be done with a dumbbell or a light bar. It can be done seated with the forearms resting on the thighs, palms up with the wrists hanging over the end of your knees, or standing at a hyperextension bench with the forearms resting on the pad at about waist level. Hold the dumbbell or bar with a palms-up grip. Perform the exercise by flexing your wrists.

Remind your client: • Do not allow the weight to roll off your fingers as you see the exercise performed by some athletes. The only action is at the wrist joint.

Trainer's pointer: • If your client has experienced elbow tendinitis, he might find this exercise difficult to do without pain. Still, this exercise is beneficial for those with elbow tendinitis. Therefore, try having the client perform the movement with no weight. If he can do so without pain, try a half-pound or one-pound weight and gradually work up to something more challenging.

WRIST EXTENSION

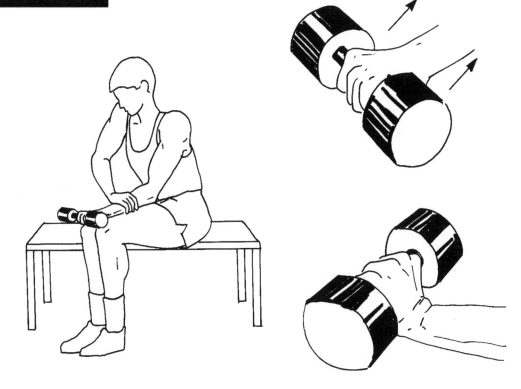

Objective:	To flex the wrist back.
How to do it:	Like wrist flexion, this exercise can be done seated with the forearms resting on the thighs, or standing at a hyperextension bench. Grasp a dumbbell or a light bar with a palms-down grip. Perform the exercise by flexing the wrists to raise the resistance.
Remind your client:	• This exercise is more difficult than wrist flexion. Perform it slowly and deliberately without using momentum.
	• Do not move the forearm. The only action is at the wrist joint.
Trainer's pointer:	• If your client has experienced elbow tendinitis, he might find this exercise difficult to do without pain. Still, this exercise is beneficial for those with elbow tendinitis. Therefore, try having the client perform the movement with no weight. If he can do so without pain, try a half-pound or one-pound weight and gradually work up to something more challenging.

HAMMER CURL

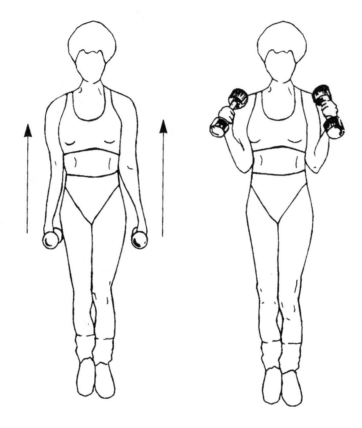

Objective: To bend the elbow.

How to do it: Stand or sit on a bench with a back support, and grasp a dumbbell in each hand, palms facing the body. Keeping the upper arms against your torso, curl the weight by flexing at the elbow joint. Raise the dumbbells to shoulder level. Lower and repeat. Your palms should be facing in during the entire exercise.

Remind your client: • This exercise is very similar to the dumbbell curl. The difference is that you do not rotate your palms so that your little fingers are higher than your thumbs during the exercise. Rather, you maintain the palms-facing-you position throughout.

Trainer's pointer: • Make sure your client keeps her upper arms firmly against her body.

LYING LEG CURL

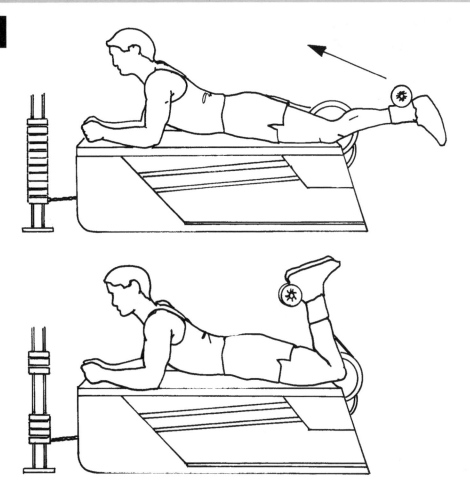

Objective:	To lift the weight stack by flexing the knee.
How to do it:	Lie face down on a leg curl machine. Adjust the machine's pads so that your knees are just off the edge of the bench and the ankle pad hits you at the Achilles tendon. Place your feet under the ankle pad. Before initiating any knee flexion, tighten your gluteus and transverse abdominis. Raise the stack by flexing your knees.
Remind your client:	• Do not rest when your leg or legs are straight. Lift and lower the weight in a controlled fashion.
	• Keep your hip joint out of the exercise by keeping your transverse abdominis and glutes tight and your pelvis pressed against the bench. Flex and extend only at the knee.
	• Concentrate on keeping your feet from turning out. Keep them straight, with the balls of the feet in line with the knees.
Trainer's pointers:	• Give your client a tactile cue for activating the glutes and transverse abdominis by placing your fingers on these muscles and having him activate them before he does the exercise. Ask him if he can feel the difference between these muscles being flexed and relaxed, and remind him that they should feel activated the whole time he's doing the exercise.
	• I strongly recommend that you have your client do these one leg at a time occasionally for balanced development.
	• It will be difficult for your client to keep his glutes tight, but encourage him to try.

STANDING LEG CURL

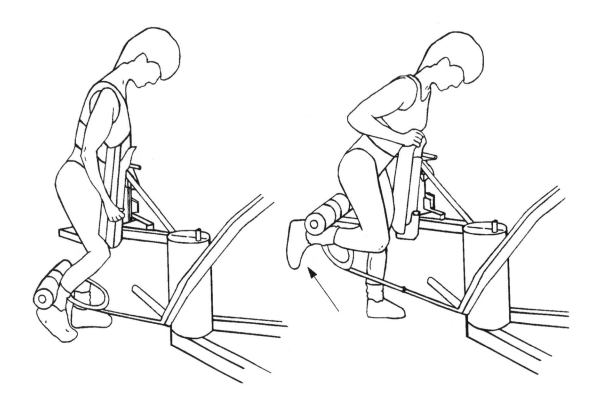

Objective: To flex the knee.

How to do it: Stand in front of a standing leg curl machine with your ankles behind the pad. Activate your gluteus and transverse abdominis. You should keep these muscles tight the entire time you're doing the exercise. Keeping the knee of your supporting leg soft, lift the stack by flexing the knee of your working leg.

Remind your client: • This is a single-joint movement. Don't twist at the waist or rock your pelvis.

• Try to keep the foot of the working leg straight, not turned out.

Trainer's pointer: • Constantly monitor the position of the pelvis and the activation of the gluteus and transverse abdominis. If you notice that your client can't execute the movement without arching her back, reduce the resistance.

BARBELL DEADLIFT

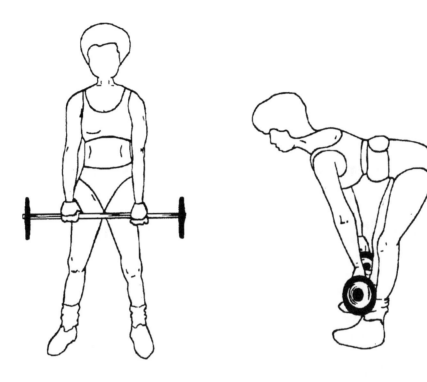

Objective:	To bend forward at the waist by flexing the hip.
How to do it:	Grasp a barbell with an evenly spaced palms-down grip. Create your four-finger space by lifting your rib cage and pulling your shoulder blades in line with your spinal column. Tighten your gluteus and transverse abdominis. Keeping your head up and your back flat, bend forward at the waist until the bar is just below your knees. Return to the starting position. Repeat for the required number of repetitions.
Remind your client:	• Keep your back flat.
	• The bar must stay extremely close to your body.
	• Your knees should be soft, but don't flex and extend them.
	• Keep your transverse abdominis and gluteus tight.
	• Go through a full range of motion. Straighten your back completely on every repetition.
Trainer's pointers:	• Watch your client's back. If it rounds, go through the posture checklist (chapter 5, p. 46) with her again.
	• Make sure your client keeps the resistance close to her body. Suggest that she imagine shaving the front of the legs with the bar.
	• Make sure this movement is done slowly and under control. No ballistics or jerking!
	• Beginners should perform this exercise with dumbbells to avoid the risk of elbow tendinitis.
	• **Caution:** This is an advanced exercise that might be risky for those with weak abdominals and/or excess abdominal weight.

DUMBBELL DEADLIFT

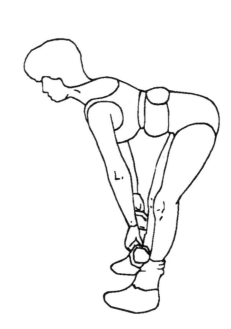

Objective: To bend forward at the waist by flexing the hip.

How to do it: While standing, grasp two dumbbells (one in each hand). Hold the resistance in front of your thighs, palms down. Create your four-finger space between your pelvis and rib cage and pull your shoulder blades in line with your spinal column. Tighten your gluteus and transverse abdominis. Keeping your head up, bend forward at the waist until the resistance is just below your knees. Return to the starting position. Repeat for the required number of repetitions.

Remind your client:
- Keep your back flat. Check your posture. If it is correct, you will automatically have a flat back.
- The resistance must stay extremely close to your body.
- Do not flex and extend your elbows.
- Do not turtle.

Trainer's pointers:
- Watch your client's back. If it rounds, go through the posture checklist (chapter 5, p. 46) with her again.
- Make sure your client keeps the resistance next to the body. Suggest that she shave the front of her legs with the dumbbells.
- **Caution:** This is an advanced exercise that might be risky for those with weak abdominals and/or excess abdominal weight.

BACK EXTENSION ON FLOOR

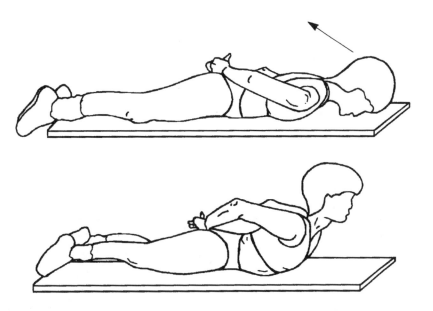

Objective:	To lift the chest off the mat or floor.
How to do it:	Lie face down on the floor. Place your hands behind your back. Lift your chest off the mat or floor. Return to the starting position.
Remind your client:	• Do not hyperextend your neck. Keep your chin down so that your neck is in line with the spine.
	• Do not twist your spine.
	• Maintain your pace. Lift and lower your chest at a steady rate.
Trainer's pointers:	• Stabilize your client's pelvis by placing your hands on her thighs.
	• To make this exercise more challenging, have your client raise her arms over her head.
	• To make this exercise easier, have your client place her hands at her sides, in contact with the ground, and lift her chest while straightening her arms.
	• Advanced trainers can do this exercise on the leg curl machine by setting the pad so that the feet can be comfortably placed under them.

LEG EXTENSION

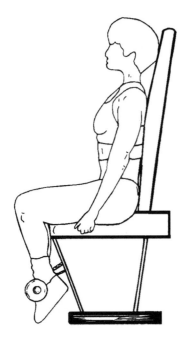 

Objective: To straighten the knee while keeping the hip relaxed.

How to do it: Sit on the leg extension station of a universal or similar machine with your knees bent and your feet behind the pads of the leg extension attachment, which should hit you at the ankle joint. Extend your legs by straightening them at the knee joint. While generally done two legs at a time, this exercise can also be done one leg at a time for greater isolation and balanced development.

Remind your client:
- Try to actively flex the front of your thighs when the working leg is in the extended position. One good way to focus on this is to hold the peak contraction for a count of one.

- Keep your upper body relaxed. Do not allow your body to come up out of the chair or your hips to rise.

- Make sure that the machine, chair, or bench provides adequate back support.

Trainer's pointer:
- Make sure your client keeps her upper body relaxed. If she's bouncing around in the chair, she's trying to use her hip flexors to move the resistance. Reduce the weight.

BARBELL SQUAT

Objective:	To lower the body as if sitting in a chair.
How to do it:	Stand in front of a squat rack with the bar at the appropriate height to allow you to unrack it without rising on your toes or bending over. Go under the bar and unrack it, maintaining a palms-forward grip, holding the bar behind your head and resting it on your shoulders. Step away from the rack and stand with your feet approximately shoulder-width apart. Shift body weight back to heels. This should cause a slightly forward lean, which is fine provided the back stays flat. Bend at the knees by flexing your hips, lowering the glutes behind the heels. When your thighs are parallel to the floor and your knees are flexed at 90 degrees, immediately push back up to the starting position. Don't rest when your legs are straight. Ascend and descend at a controlled, steady pace, up to a count of two and down to a count of three or four. When you've finished the designated number of reps, come to a complete stop.

Remind your client:

- Keep body weight back on the heels.

- Make sure you keep the bar firmly on the back of your shoulders. Do not allow the bar to roll down your back.

- Always squat with a spotter and understand the proper method for bailing out.

- It is suggested that you wear a weight belt during squats and lunges.

- Be sure to initiate the exercise by flexing at the hip, not the knee. Drop your hips as if you were sitting down on an imaginary bench. It may feel like you are sticking your rear end out, and if it does, you're doing it right.

- Keep your head up, back straight, and abdominals tight.

- Never go lower than the point where thighs are parallel with the floor; that is, knees should never be flexed at an angle smaller than 90 degrees.

Trainer's pointers:

- Have your client activate the glutes and transverse abdominis before descending.

- Make sure your client's knees stay directly over her feet, not in front of them.

- Watch for the beginner's tendency not to flex at the hip joint, but only at the knee, which places the knee in hyperflexion. If your client's knees move in front of the balls of her feet stop her and review form.

DUMBBELL SQUAT

Objective:	To lower the body as if sitting in a chair.
How to do it:	Stand with your feet approximately shoulder-width apart and hold a dumbbell in each hand. Shift your weight back to your heels. With your arms straight and at your sides, descend by flexing at the hip and then flexing at the knee until your thighs are parallel with the ground. Return to the starting position. Repeat for the required number of repetitions.
Remind your client:	• Be sure to initiate the movement at your hip joint, not the knees. Think about dropping your gluteus behind your heels.
	• Keep your weight back on your heels.
	• Keep the dumbbells at your sides.
Trainer's pointers:	• Have your client activate the gluteus and transverse abdominis before descending.
	• Make sure your client's knees stay directly over her feet, not in front of them.
	• Watch for the beginner's tendency not to flex at the hip joint, but only at the knee, which places the knee in hyperflexion. If your client's knees move in front of the balls of her feet stop her and review form.

LEG PRESS

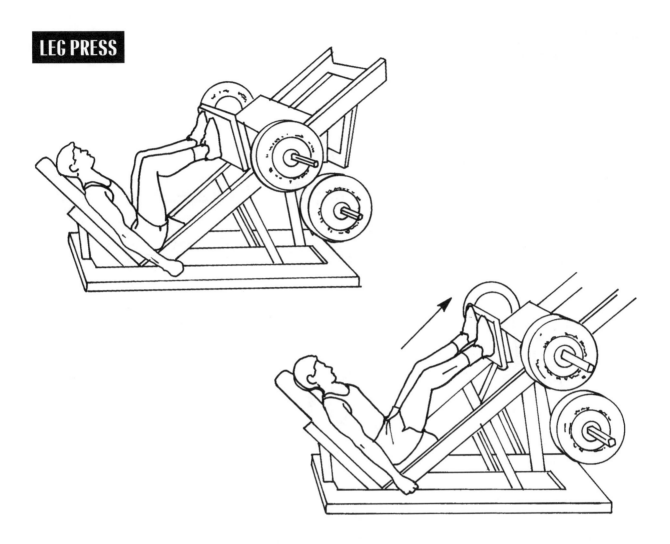

Objective:	To press the weight stack up by straightening the leg at the knee.
How to do it:	Sit on the seat of a leg press machine. Before beginning, check the seat's position. It should be positioned so that you are able to place your feet flat on the machine's platform without hyperextending your knees or flexing your hips. Unrack the stack, and lower it under control until your legs are at approximately 90 degrees of flexion. Press the stack up. Do not pause at the top. Repeat for the required number of repetitions.
Remind your client:	• Don't hyperextend your knees when pressing up the stack. They should retain a slight softness even when the stack is pressed up.
	• Keep your upper body relaxed.
	• Keep your feet on the platform.
	• Make sure that the knees are aligned over the feet. They should not collapse in or flare out.
	• Do not pause at the top of the movement.
Trainer's pointers:	• Advise your client to use caution when adding or removing plates from a loaded leg press machine. Alternate removing plates from each side. *Never* remove them all from one side at a time because the machine could tip over.
	• Vary the width between the clients' feet to target different areas of the quadriceps.

BARBELL LUNGE

Objective:	To lower the body toward the ground by flexing both knees and the hips.
How to do it:	Stand in front of a squat rack with the bar at the appropriate height to allow you to unrack it without rising on your toes or bending over. Go under the bar and unrack it. Step away from the rack. Keeping one leg slightly in front of your body, extend one leg behind and slightly (about 30 degrees) away from the center of your body with the foot flexed. Maintaining good posture, lower your body by flexing both knees 90 degrees. Return to the starting position and repeat the required number of repetitions.
Remind your client:	• Be sure to flex both knees. Beginners tend to flex only the front knee, causing it to go beyond the ball of the foot, a potentially dangerous move.
	• Keep the gluteus tight. Think of them as a sponge and squeeze.
	• Be sure to exert enough force with the arms and shoulders to keep the bar from rolling down the back.
Trainer's pointers:	• Observe your client from the side to make sure she is flexing both knees. There is a tendency not to flex the back one, placing the front knee in a dangerous hyperflexed position.
	• Make sure your client has her body weight distributed on her front heel and back toe.

DUMBBELL LUNGE

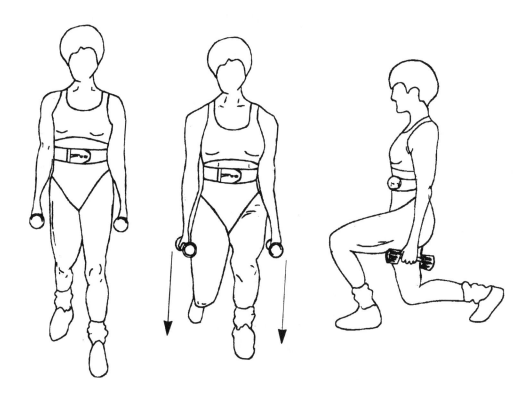

Objective:	To lower the body toward the ground by flexing both knees and the hips.
How to do it:	Hold a dumbbell in each hand, palms facing your body and arms beside your body. Keep your head up and back straight. Extend your leg back and slightly to the outside (about 30 degrees away from the center of the body) with the foot flexed. Maintaining good posture, lower your body by flexing both knees 90 degrees. Return to the starting position and repeat the required number of repetitions.
Remind your client:	• Be sure to keep the dumbbells close to your body, in line with your ears. If you allow your arms to travel forward, this will change your center of gravity and cause you to lean forward, putting a great deal of stress on your low back. • Flex both knees, but do not let the back knee touch the ground. • Do not look down! If you do, you will bend forward, which stresses the low back. • Keep your four-finger space between your pelvis and rib cage. • The front knee should *never* go farther forward than the ball of the front foot. • Keep the body's weight back on the front heel and rear toe. • Keep the glutes tight throughout the exercise.
Trainer's pointers:	• Watch the tendency to flex only the front leg at the knee, while flexing the back leg only at the hip. • Have your client activate her glutes and transverse abdominis before beginning the movement. • Make sure your client keeps her scapula in line with the spinal column.

Rotator Cuff

Some general notes about the rotator cuff: As noted in the text, the rotator cuff is one of the most important and most neglected group of muscles in the body. Most weightlifters will develop rotator cuff problems unless they work on strength and flexibility in this area. As your client does the rotator cuff exercises, be aware of the following:

1. Is your client experiencing any clicking or popping at the shoulder joint? I find it helpful to place my hands on the shoulders to feel for these symptoms. If so, try to adjust the position of the scapula (by having the client pull it down) or the upper arm. If the clicking and popping continues, try reducing the weight.

2. Is your client experiencing any pain or discomfort in the shoulder or elsewhere while doing these exercises? If so, try reducing the weight or doing the exercise without any additional weight at all. If the exercise is too easy without added weight, try using some manual resistance.

3. How much range of motion does your client have at the shoulder joint? Does it differ between sides of the body? Can he touch his fingers together between his shoulder blades? (See illustration.) This information will help you refine the client's workout.

4. Is your client a lot stronger on one side than the other? If so, you need to concentrate on the weak side. You might also find it necessary to use a lighter weight on the weaker side until you and your client are able to correct this imbalance.

WINDMILL

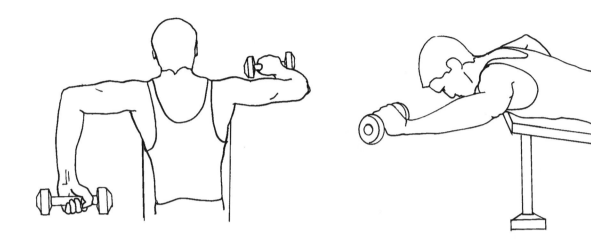

Objective: To rotate the upper arms back and forth.

How to do it: Hold a light dumbbell in each hand. Lie face down on a bench with your head hanging over the edge. With your upper arms at 90 degrees to your body, and your elbows flexed 90 degrees, rotate your arms back and forth until the dumbbells are alternately level with your head and the bench. Your neck should be straight; your head should be in line with your spinal column. Your shoulder blades should be in line with your spinal column.

Remind your client: • Keep your arms and elbows at 90 degree angles.

• Keep your head up.

Trainer's pointer: • This is an advanced exercise. It is helpful in correcting round-shoulder posture, but in order to do it in correct form, the client must have a little background in weight training and the body awareness that comes with it.

LYING L

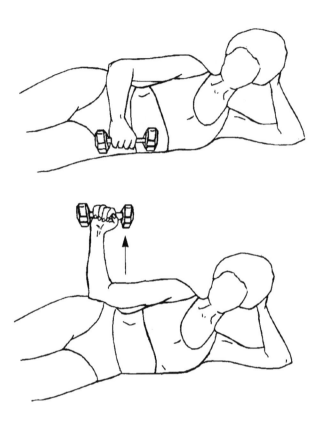

Objective: To rotate the upper arm at the shoulder joint.

How to do it: Lie on your side on the floor. Support your head with one hand (elbow bent). Hold a light dumbbell in the other hand. Place the upper arm of this hand firmly against your body with the elbow flexed at 90 degrees. Keeping your wrist straight and maintaining this 90 degree angle at the elbow joint, move the dumbbell up toward the ceiling, then back until it is line with your body. After performing the designated number of repetitions, switch sides.

Remind your client:
- Keep the wrist straight.
- Keep your neck relaxed. Don't turtle.
- Keep your scapula pulled down and in line with your spinal column.
- Keep the elbow in contact with the hip bone.

Trainer's pointers:
- Make sure the client is doing this exercise slowly and under control. There is a tendency to throw the weight up and down.
- Watch the wrist for undesirable flexion and extension.

LYING INTERNAL/EXTERNAL ROTATION

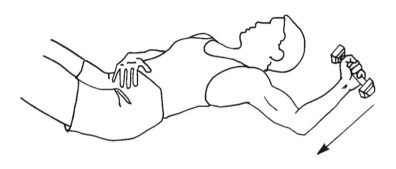

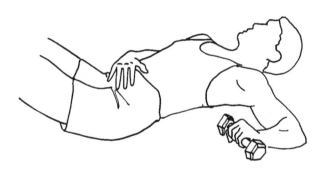

Objective:	To rotate the upper arm.
How to do it:	Lie on your back on the floor with your knees bent. Hold a light dumbbell in one hand. Your upper arm should be at a 90-degree angle to your body, and your elbow should be flexed 90 degrees. Maintaining these two 90-degree angles, move the dumbbell as far in both directions as you can comfortably and under full control while keeping your shoulder on the ground. Do the required number of repetitions, then repeat on the other side.
Remind your client:	• Keep your upper arm at a 90-degree angle. Do not allow this to straighten.
	• Keep the wrist rigid.
	• Keep your neck and shoulders relaxed.
	• Keep your scapula in line with your spinal column.
Trainer's pointer:	• Each client's range of motion on this exercise will be different. Some may be able to lower the dumbbell all the way to the floor in both directions with their shoulders on the ground. Monitor the range of motion and try to work toward gradual improvement.

DUMBBELL SHOULDER PRESS

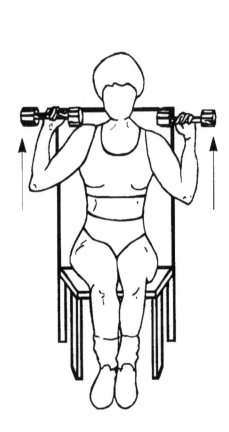
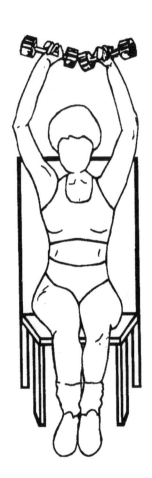

Objective:	To press the dumbbells overhead by straightening the arms.
How to do it:	Sit on a bench with a back support. Hold one dumbbell in each hand, palms facing forward. Begin with the dumbbells at shoulder level and press them up overhead. The dumbbells should come together at the top of the movement.
Remind your client:	• Make sure you bring the dumbbells all the way down to your shoulders on each rep.
	• The dumbbells should travel on the same plane with your head. Don't allow your upper arms to move forward during the exercise.
	• Remember to control your wrists. Do not allow them to flex and extend or otherwise flop around. Keep them straight.
	• Keep your back against the bench.
Trainer's pointers:	• Ask your client if she is experiencing any clicking or popping in her shoulders. Place your hands on her shoulders to feel for anything unusual. If clicking or popping is a problem, have your client try doing the exercise with her hands in a neutral position (palms facing each other).
	• Make sure your client keeps her neck relaxed.

BARBELL SHOULDER PRESS

Objective: To press the barbell overhead by straightening the arms.

How to do it: Sit on a stable chair with a back support. Grasp the bar slightly wider than shoulder-width apart with palms facing forward. On a count of three, have your trainer or spotter give you a lift off. Lower the bar under control to about ear level in front of your head. Press the bar up by straightening your arms.

Remind your client:
- This is a multijoint exercise. Be sure to lower the upper arms as well as flexing and extending at the elbows.
- Keep the wrists as straight as possible.
- Don't turtle!

Trainer's pointers:
- Be sure that your client maintains good posture (for example, four-finger space between the pelvis and rib cage).
- Watch for uneven arm extension. It's not uncommon for the weaker side to lag behind.
- While it is extremely important that your client go through a full range of motion, there is little to be gained, and much potential harm to the shoulder, from lowering the bar below ear level.

DUMBBELL SIDE RAISE

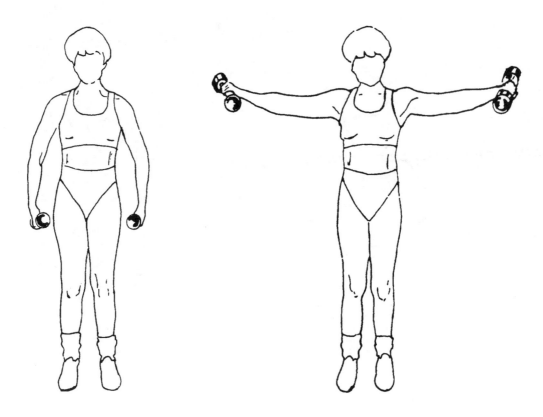

Objective:	To lift the upper arms away from the body.
How to do it:	This exercise may be done seated or standing. Hold one dumbbell in each hand, palms facing your sides. Lift your arms out to your sides until they are at shoulder level. Lower and repeat.
Remind your client:	• Keep your elbow joints soft, but straight. The action is only at the shoulder joint. • Do not turtle. Your upper trapezius should stay relaxed.
Trainer's pointer:	• Be alert for clicking and popping in the shoulder joint. Ask your client if there's any clicking or popping and place your hands on the shoulder to check. If you find any, try adjusting the position of the upper arms by moving them forward or back. Having your client depress her scapula might help. You should also reduce the weight. If this doesn't work, eliminate this exercise until your client's neck and shoulder flexibility improves and it can be done without the snap, crackle, and pop.

DUMBBELL FRONT RAISE

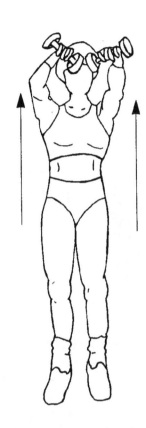

Objective:	To lift the arms in front of the body.
How to do it:	Stand holding a dumbbell in each hand with palms down and directly in front of your thighs. Keeping your good posture, with your elbows slightly bent, raise your arms in front of your body.
Remind your client:	• Don't rock or twist your body. Your spine should stay still and relaxed. The shoulder is the only axis of rotation.
	• Keep the wrist rigid.
	• Do not flex and extend the elbow. Keep it frozen.
	• Keep the knees soft and relaxed.
Trainer's pointers:	• Be sure your client maintains good posture (for example, four-finger space between the pelvis and rib cage).
	• If your client begins rocking her body, suggest that she soften the knees.
	• This exercise may also be done by alternating the arms.

BENT DUMBBELL RAISE

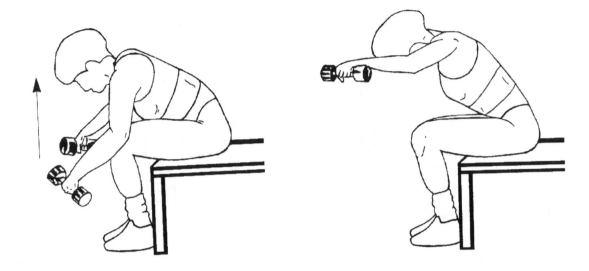

Objective: To lift the arms at a 45-degree angle to the body.

How to do it: Sit on a chair or a bench. Hold one dumbbell in each hand. Bend forward at the waist. With your upper arms at approximately a 45-degree angle to your head, and your elbows slightly bent, place the front ends of the dumbbells together. Lift your arms out to your sides. Concentrate on keeping your upper arms in the proper plane. Lower and repeat. When viewed from above, you should resemble the letter 'Y,' not the letter 'T.'

Remind your client:
- Keep your elbows slightly bent but rigid. The action is at the shoulder joint.
- Do not allow your wrists to flop around.
- Do not move your body at the spine or neck. Keep your body relaxed and move only at the shoulder joint.
- If you feel the need to rock your body up and down during the exercise, the weight you are using is too heavy.
- Lift your upper arms until they are in line with your head and no higher.
- Never do this exercise standing, unless your back is supported.
- Maintain your four-finger space between your pelvis and rib cage—don't slouch!

Trainer's pointers:
- Watch the tendency to move the upper arms back in line with the shoulders rather than the ears. When viewed from above, the client should look like a 'Y.' Place your hands on the upper arms if necessary to keep them in the proper plane.
- Make sure your client keeps her scapula depressed and her rib cage lifted.
- The challenges here are to keep the back flat and straight and to keep the neck relaxed. Pay particular attention to these critical form points.

CABLE SIDE RAISE

Objective:	To lift the upper arm out to the side.

How to do it: Stand with your right side facing a machine with a low pulley. Grasp the handle with your left hand. Stand up straight with the handle in front of your body. Bend your left elbow slightly. Keeping the shoulder blades pulled down and the left elbow rigid, lift the left arm out to the side until it is at shoulder level. Repeat for the required number of repetitions. Turn and work the right shoulder with the handle in the right hand.

Remind your client:
- Keep the spine straight and relaxed. Don't rock back and forth, twist, or rotate.
- Don't turtle. Keep the shoulder blades pulled down.
- Don't flex and extend the elbow. Keep it rigid to keep the focus on the shoulder.
- Keep the wrist rigid.

Trainer's pointers:
- Make sure that your client maintains the four-finger space and keeps the shoulder blades pulled down.
- Check for clicking and popping in the working shoulder. If you detect it, suggest that your client re-adjust the shoulder blade by pulling it down.
- If your client rocks her body, suggest that she soften the knees more.
- Watch for and strongly discourage turtleing.

CABLE FRONT RAISE

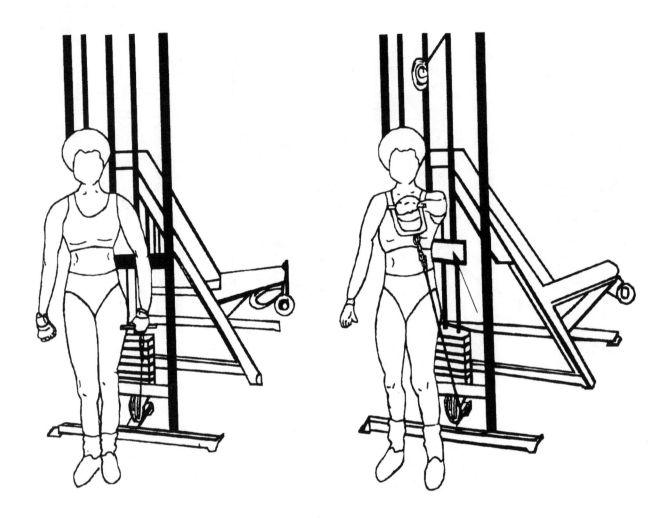

Objective:	To lift the arm in front of the body.
How to do it:	Stand with your back to a machine with a low handle. Grasp the handle with your palm down. Keeping your posture correct and your elbows slightly bent, raise your arm in front of your body.
Remind your client:	• Don't rock or twist your body. Your spine should stay still and relaxed.
	• Keep the wrist rigid.
	• Do not flex or extend the elbow.
Trainer's pointers:	• Make sure that the shoulder, elbow, and wrist are in the same plane.
	• If your client begins rocking her body, suggest that she soften the knees more.

BENT CABLE RAISE

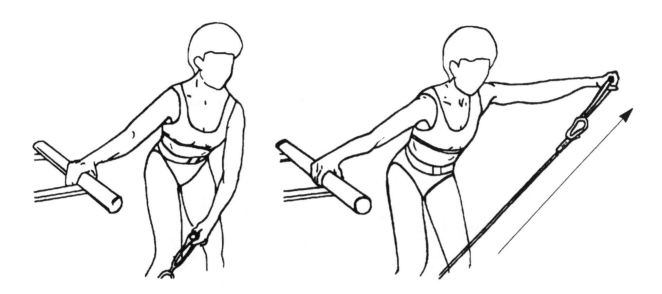

Objective:	To lift the upper arm out to the side while bending forward at the hip and keeping the elbow rigid.

How to do it: Stand with your right side facing a machine with a low pulley. Grasp the handle with your left hand. Flex the knees and bend forward at the waist. Support your body weight by placing your right hand on the machine. Grasp the handle in front of your body. Bend your left elbow slightly. Keeping the shoulder blades pulled down and the left elbow rigid, lift the left arm out to the side until it is at shoulder level. Repeat for the required number of repetitions. Turn and work the right shoulder with the handle in the right hand.

Remind your client:
- Keep the spine straight and relaxed. Don't rock back and forth, twist, or rotate. The spine should stay rigid.
- Don't turtle.
- Don't flex or extend the elbow. Keep it rigid and focus on the shoulder.
- Keep the wrist rigid.
- Keep the knees soft.

Trainer's pointers:
- Make sure that your client maintains both good posture and her forward stance.
- Check for clicking and popping in the working shoulder. If you detect it, suggest that your client re-adjust her shoulder blade by pulling it down.
- If your client rocks her body, suggest that she soften the knees.
- Watch for and strongly discourage turtleing.
- Elbow flexion and extension can be a major problem. If your client can't do the exercise without flexing her elbow, reduce the amount of weight.

UPRIGHT ROW

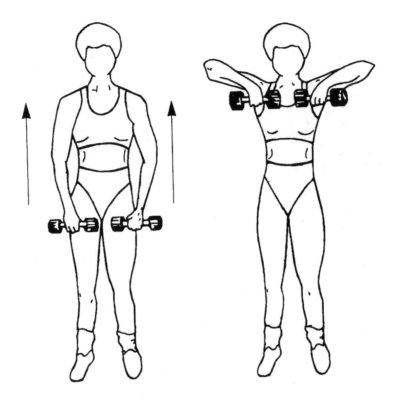

Objective: To lift the upper arms, leading with the elbows.

How to do it: Grasp a bar or dumbbells with a palms-down grip. Place your hands about shoulder-width apart or closer, whichever is more comfortable. Stand with your back straight and knees soft. Keeping the bar or dumbbells very close to your body, pull the resistance up until it is under your chin. At this point, your elbows should be just below ear level. Lower back to the starting position.

Remind your client:
- Do not swing your upper body. It should remain still.
- Use moderate amounts of weight for this exercise.
- Lead with your elbows. Do not shrug your shoulders toward your ears.
- Keep your knees soft and relaxed.

Trainer's pointer:
- Some clients who have trouble doing this exercise with a bar can do it successfully with dumbbells because the weight is lighter and dumbbells allow more adjustment in the plane of motion. Also, they place less stress on the wrists and forearms.

BARBELL SHRUG

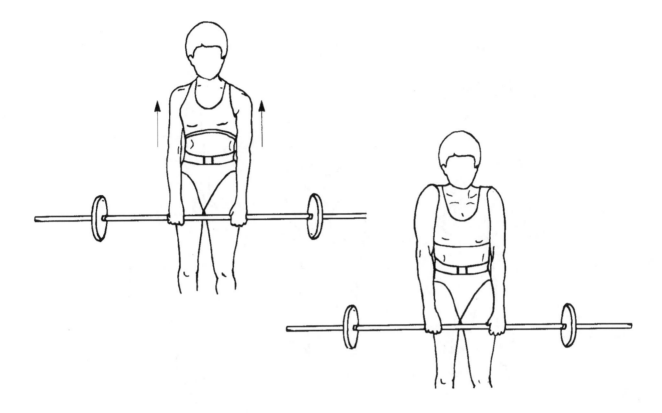

Objective:	To pull the shoulders up toward the ears while keeping the arms straight.
How to do it:	Stand while holding a bar in front of you. Your hands should be approximately shoulder-width apart. Keeping your elbows frozen, shrug your shoulders up toward your ears.
Remind your client:	• Don't flex or extend the elbows.
	• Don't roll the shoulders back and forth. The shoulders should elevate, not rotate.
	• Keep the knees soft and relaxed.
	• Keep the bar extremely close to the body.
Trainer's pointers:	• Be sure that your client maintains good posture.
	• Watch for elbow flexion and extension.

DUMBBELL SHRUG

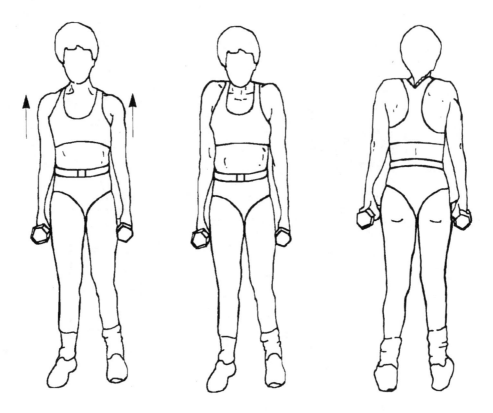

Objective:	To elevate the shoulders up toward the ears while keeping the arms straight.
How to do it:	Stand while holding a pair of dumbbells, one in each hand, at your sides. Keeping your elbows rigid, shrug your shoulders up toward your ears.
Remind your client:	• Don't flex and extend the elbows.
	• Don't roll the shoulders back and forth. The shoulders should elevate, not rotate.
	• Keep the knees soft and relaxed.
	• Keep the dumbbells close to the body.
Trainer's pointers:	• Be sure that your client maintains good posture.
	• Watch for elbow flexion and extension.
	• Dumbbell shrugs may also be done with the dumbbells in front of your body.

LYING SIDE RAISE (HORIZONTAL ABDUCTION)

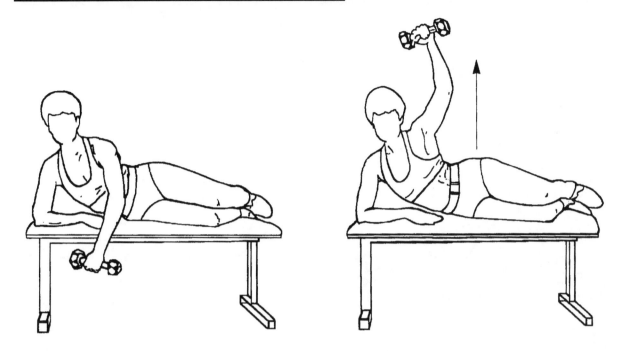

Objective: To lift the arm out to the side until it is in line with the body while keeping the elbow stationary.

How to do it: Lie on your right side on a bench or on the floor with your knees slightly bent and your upper body resting on your right forearm. Your pelvis should be facing squarely forward. Hold a dumbbell in your left hand, palm down. Your left elbow should be slightly bent, approximately in line with your shoulder and facing out. Keeping the scapula depressed and the elbow stationary, lift your arm until the elbow is in line with your head. Return to the beginning position and repeat for the specified number of repetitions. Switch positions so that you are lying on your left side. Perform the same number of repetitions on the right side.

Remind your client:
- Don't allow your body to roll toward one side or the other.
- Your entire body should be facing forward.
- Keep the wrist rigid.
- Keep the neck relaxed.
- Keep the shoulder blades pulled down.

Trainer's pointers:
- Be sure that your client maintains good posture. There should be no forward spinal flexion.
- Watch carefully for elbow flexion and extension. If it isn't possible for your client to do the exercise without bending the elbow, reduce the weight.
- Suggest that your client visualize her arm moving back and forth like a wing in a flying motion.
- Check for clicking and popping in the working shoulder. If clicking and popping are present, adjusting the position of the arm with relation to the body might help.
- Large or less experienced clients will find this exercise easier to do on the floor for stability.

LYING SIDE RAISE (FRONTAL ABDUCTION)

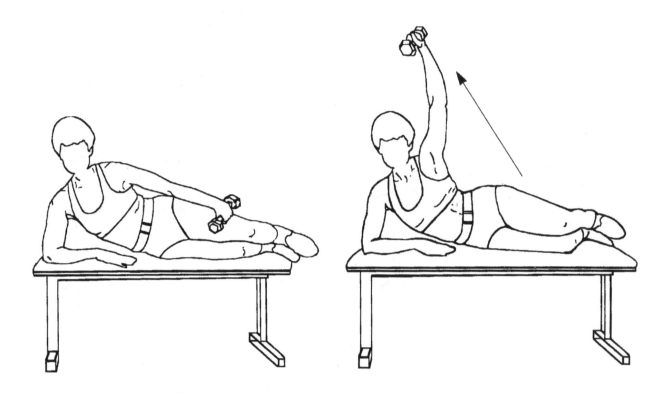

Objective: To lift the arm away from the side and toward the head.

How to do it: Lie on your right side on a bench or on the floor with your knees slightly bent. Your pelvis should be facing squarely forward. Hold a dumbbell in your left hand, palm down. Your elbow should be slightly bent. Begin with your left arm on top of your left thigh. Lift your arm up until the dumbbell is over your head. Return to beginning position and repeat for the specified number of repetitions. Switch positions so that you are lying on your left side. Perform the same number of repetitions on the right side.

Remind your client:
- Don't allow your body to roll toward one side or the other.
- Your entire body should be facing forward.
- Keep the wrist rigid.
- Keep the neck relaxed.
- Keep the shoulder blades pulled down.

Trainer's pointers:
- Be sure that your client maintains good posture.
- Suggest that your client think of her arm moving up like the hand of a clock in reverse.
- This exercise is more difficult than it looks and is recommended only for advanced clients.
- Larger or less experienced clients will find this exercise easier to do on the floor.

Triceps

TRICEPS PUSHDOWN

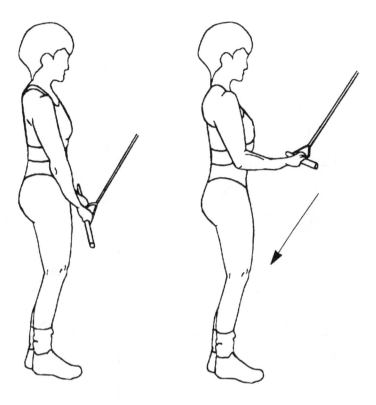

Objective: To bend and straighten the arms at the elbow while keeping the upper arm against the body.

How to do it: Stand in front of a machine with a high pulley. Grasp the overhead bar attached to the cable with palms down and thumbs on top. Keeping the upper arms firmly against and slightly in front of the center of the body, push the bar down by straightening the elbows. Allow your elbows to flex 90 degrees and no more. Repeat for the required number of repetitions.

Remind your client:
- *Do not* allow your upper arm to move during the exercise. Keep your upper arm glued to the side of your body!
- Do not shrug your shoulders up toward your ears. Try to keep your neck relaxed.
- Focus on flexing and extending your elbows.

Trainer's pointers:
- Make sure your client moves the resistance by flexing and extending at the elbow. Some have a tendency to try to use the shoulder during this exercise.
- A V-shaped bar is easier on the forearms and wrists than a straight bar.
- Watch for the tendency to bend the wrist at the top of the movement. Bending the wrist should be avoided.

SINGLE TRICEPS PULLDOWN

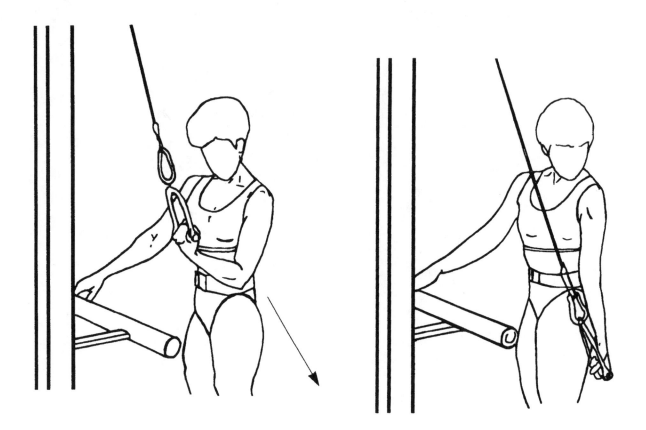

Objective: To straighten the arm at the elbow joint while keeping the upper arm against the body.

How to do it: Stand facing a machine with a high pulley. Attach the small handle. Grasp the handle with your left hand in a palms-up grip. Keeping the upper arm firmly against the body, straighten the arm at the elbow. Return to the beginning position (90 degrees of elbow flexion). Repeat for the required number of repetitions. Switch arms and perform the same number of repetitions on the right arm.

Remind your client:
- Don't rock your body. The only axis of rotation is the elbow.
- Keep the upper arm firmly against your body.
- Keep your neck relaxed.
- Don't flex and extend the wrist.
- Don't rotate at the spine.

Trainer's pointers:
- The angle at the elbow joint should not be less than 90 degrees to maintain pressure on the triceps.
- You might suggest that your client place the hand of her nonworking arm on her working triceps to increase focus and activation.
- This exercise may also be done with a palms-down grip.
- Watch for the tendency to bend the wrist at the top of the movement. Bending the wrist should be avoided.

LYING BARBELL TRICEPS EXTENSION

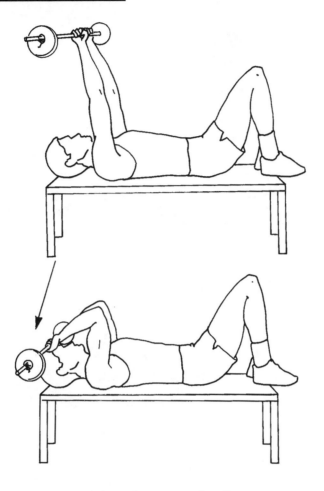

Objective: To bend and straighten the arms at the elbow.

How to do it: Lie face up on a flat bench. Your knees should be bent and your feet should be flat on the bench. Grasp a straight or curled bar in your hands. Straighten your arms so that the weight is over your head and your upper arms are at about nipple level. Your upper arms should be at a 90-degree angle to your body and to the bench. Keeping your upper arms stationary, lower the weight to your forehead by flexing your elbows. Straighten your arms and repeat.

Remind your client:
- Do not move your upper arms. Concentrate on moving at the elbow joint and flexing the triceps. This exercise is sometimes called a "skull crusher."
- Keep your elbows in line and in the same plane with your shoulders.
- Do not arch your back. Make sure your feet are up on the bench.

Trainer's pointers:
- Reassure your client by placing your hands just above and to the sides of his head. Constantly monitor the position of the elbows to make sure they are in line with the shoulders.
- Watch for the tendency to flex and extend the wrists.
- A curled bar is easier on the wrists and forearms than a straight bar.
- To keep his elbows in line with his shoulders, have your client visualize holding a ball between his elbows.

LYING DUMBBELL TRICEPS EXTENSION

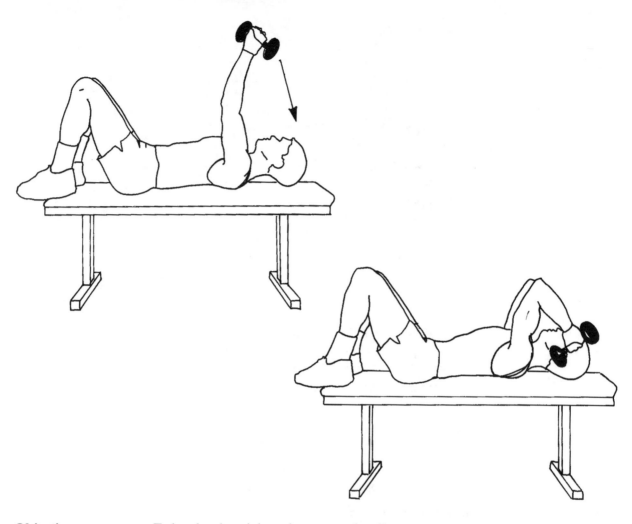

Objective: To bend and straighten the arms at the elbow.

How to do it: Lie on your back on a flat bench with your feet up on the bench. Grasp one dumbbell in each hand. Straighten your arms with your palms in and your elbows in the same plane as your shoulders. Your arms should be at a 90-degree angle to your body and the bench. Lower the dumbbells to ear level by flexing at the elbow. Return to the start position by straightening, but not hyperextending your elbows.

Remind your client:
- Do not move your upper arms. Keep them at a 90-degree angle to your upper body.
- Keep your elbows in line with your shoulders. Do not allow them to flare out away from your body.
- Do not flex, extend, or deviate the wrist.

Trainer's pointers:
- Spot the client by placing your hands on the ends of the dumbbells. Don't take resistance off, rather, reassure your client that you will be there to take the dumbbells if he needs you to.
- Watch for the tendency to bend the wrist at the top of the movement. Bending the wrist should be avoided.
- To keep his elbows in line with his shoulders, have your client visualize holding a ball between his elbows.

SEATED TRICEPS EXTENSION

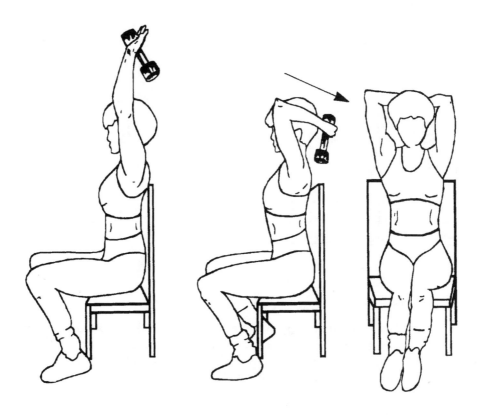

Objective: To bend and straighten the arms at the elbow.

How to do it: Sit in a chair or on a bench with a back support. Grasp one dumbbell in both hands with your fingers around the plate at one end. Straighten your arms so the weight is over your head and your upper arms are next to your ears. Keeping your upper arms stationary, lower the weight behind your head to the back of your neck by flexing only at your elbow joints. Straighten your arms and repeat.

Remind your client:
- Do not move your upper arms. Concentrate on flexing the triceps.
- The only action should be at the elbow joint.
- Keep your elbows next to your head.
- If your upper arms move forward, you might whack yourself in the head.

Trainer's pointers:
- Your client should go through a full range of motion. Make sure she lowers the weight all the way to the base of her neck and completely straightens the elbows on each rep.
- Some clients have insufficient ROM in the shoulder joint to do this exercise correctly.
- Watch for the tendency to bend the wrist at the top of the movement. Bending the wrist should be avoided.
- To keep her elbows in line with her shoulders, have your client visualize holding a ball between her elbows.

DOUBLE SEATED TRICEPS KICKBACK

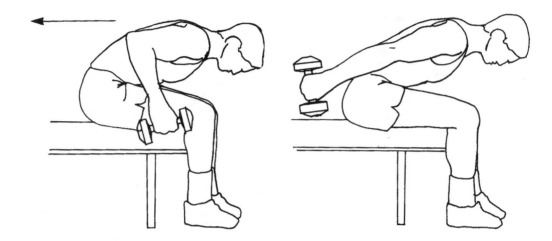

Objective: To straighten the arm at the elbow.

How to do it: Sit on the end of a bench and bend forward at the waist. Grasp a dumbbell in each hand, palms in. Flex your elbows to 90 degrees and place your upper arms against your body. Your upper arms should be parallel with the ground. Straighten your arms at the elbows. Pause a moment when your arms are straight before returning them to 90 degrees of elbow flexion.

Remind your client:
- Do not move at the shoulder joint! Keep your upper arms parallel to the ground and next to your body.
- Do not rock your body.
- Maintain the four-finger space between your pelvis and rib cage—don't slouch!

Trainer's pointers:
- Make sure your client completely straightens his arms and goes through a full range of motion.
- Watch the position of the upper arms. They tend to move forward out of the horizontal position as the client fatigues.
- Make sure your client keeps his scapula in line with his spinal column.
- Watch for the tendency to bend the wrist at the top of the movement. Bending the wrist should be avoided.

SINGLE SEATED TRICEPS KICKBACK

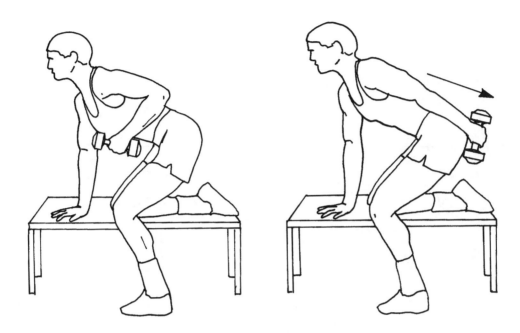

Objective:	To bend and straighten the arm at the elbow.
How to do it:	Your body should be in the same position as it is for the dumbbell row. The upper part of the working arm should be parallel with the ground. Grasp a dumbbell in one hand, bend your arm at the elbow, and place the upper arm against your body. You should begin with your elbow flexed 90 degrees, and your palm facing your body. Straighten the working arm by extending at the elbow joint. Pause, then return the elbow to the flexed position. After you have completed the designated number of repetitions, switch arms.
Remind your client:	• You must not allow the upper arm to move during this exercise. There is only one axis of rotation in this exercise, the elbow joint. • Do not do this exercise without supporting your back. • Keep your weight on your leg, not on your wrist. • Maintain the four-finger space between your pelvis and rib cage. Keep your back flat.
Trainer's pointers:	• Watch for the tendency for the upper arm to drop. It should stay parallel to the ground at a 90 degree angle. • Make sure your client fully extends his elbow. There is a tendency to cheat by not straightening the arm completely. • Make sure your client keeps his scapula in line with the spinal column, that is, keeps the four-finger space. • Check that your client keeps his weight on the leg, not the wrist. • Watch for the tendency to bend the wrist at the top of the movement. Bending the wrist should be avoided.

BENCH DIP

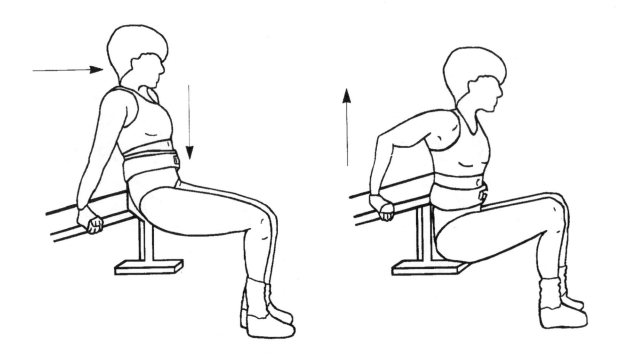

Objective: To bend and straighten the arms at the elbow.

How to do it: Sit on a bench with your hands next to your hips. With your knees bent, lift your body off the bench. Your weight should be resting on your arms, which should be straight. Lower your body by flexing at the elbows. Flex your elbows to 90 degrees. Return to the starting position by straightening your arms at the elbows.

Remind your client:
- Do not move excessively at the knee or hip joints. Remember, the main axis of rotation is the elbow, not the shoulder.
- Flex the elbows to 90 degrees.
- Keep the upper trapezius and neck relaxed.

Trainer's pointers:
- If the exercise is easy for the client with her knees bent, have her straighten them.
- Make sure your client flexes her elbows to about 90 degrees and doesn't cheat by trying to move only at the shoulder.
- Before the client begins, make sure her hands are not too far apart! The hands should be right next to her hips.

CLOSE-GRIP PUSH-UP

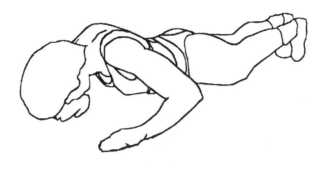

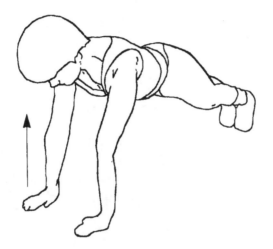

Objective: To push the body up by straightening the arms at the elbow.

How to do it: Begin on the floor or on a mat on all fours. Keeping the hands directly under the shoulders, straighten the spine by straightening the knees and tucking the toes under. The abdominals should be contracted to keep the spine firm and straight. Keeping the knees rigid, flex the elbows and lower the body as a single unit until the chest is approximately two inches from the floor.

Remind your client:
- Don't flex and extend the body at the hips or knees. Both must stay rigid.
- Keep the neck relaxed. Don't turtle!
- Don't rest all of the body's weight on the wrist. Try to distribute it across all of the fingers.
- Go through a full range of motion.

Trainer's pointers:
- Beginners can do this exercise on the knees (easy), on an incline (easier), or against the wall (easiest). If your client cannot complete the exercise through a full range of motion, have her perform an easier version.
- Spot your client by kneeling next to her and placing one hand on the front of her body at pelvic level. Use your other hand to cue her to relax the neck if needed.

CLOSE-GRIP BENCH PRESS

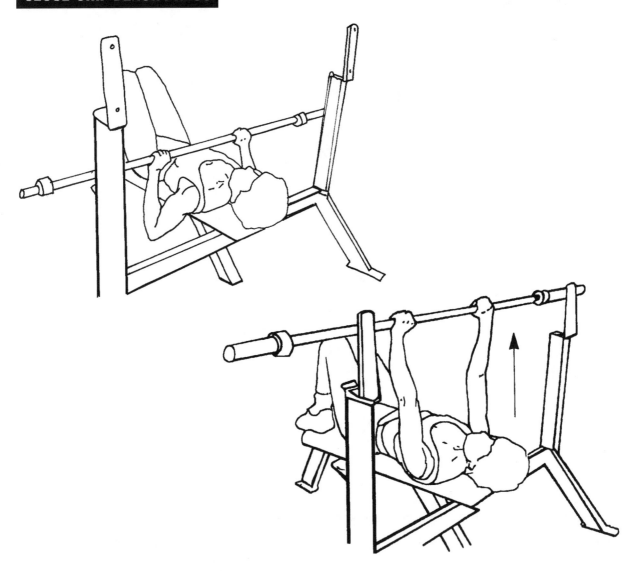

Objective: To press the bar up by straightening the arms.

How to do it: Lie on your back on a bench with bar supports. Your knees should be bent and your feet should be resting on the bench. Grasp the bar with a shoulder-width (and no wider) grip. With the help of your trainer or spotter, lift the bar off the supports. Beginning with your arms straight, lower the bar until it is an inch away from your chest. Press it up slowly and under control. Repeat for the required number of repetitions.

Remind your client:
- Keep the wrists rigid.
- Unlike the regular bench press, during the down phase of the repetition, your upper arms should stay close to the upper body. The elbows should point down, not out.

Trainer's pointers:
- Watch for uneven arm elevation.
- The bar should be at about the midpoint of the sternum throughout the exercise.
- If your client is tall or has a long torso, place another bench or step at the end of the bench for her to put her feet on.

HIP FLEXOR STRETCH

How to do it: Kneel with one knee on the ground and the opposite foot on the ground. Keeping the front foot stationary, slide the back foot back until the instep rests on the ground. Gently try to push the back foot toward the floor.

Form points: • Make sure that the knee of the front foot doesn't move forward past the instep of the foot.

• Do not rotate the spine.

LYING HIP ABDUCTOR STRETCH

How to do it: Lie on your back with your knees bent. Place your left ankle on your right knee. Place your right hand on the outside of your left knee and gently press it toward your right shoulder. Feel the stretch deep in the left glute. Hold the stretch 30 to 40 seconds. Repeat with the other side.

NOTE: This stretch effectively targets the piriformis muscle (a deep muscle that laterally rotates the femur at the hip), often a sore spot.

QUADRICEPS STRETCH

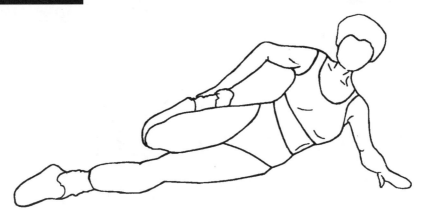

How to do it: Lie on your side on the floor. Keeping the bottom leg straight, flex the knee so that you can grasp the ankle of the top leg. Gently pull the heel of this leg toward your gluteus to stretch the quadriceps. Repeat with the other leg.

Form points:
- Make sure you don't overstretch your knee.
- Don't let your body roll.

LYING HAMSTRING STRETCH

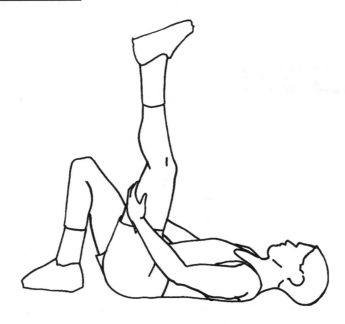

How to do it: Lie on your back with your knees bent. Straighten one leg. Place your hands behind the thigh of this leg. Keeping your gluteus down, try to bring the thigh as close to your chest as you can while keeping the leg straight. Repeat with the other leg.

Form point:
- Make sure that the gluteus stays down on the floor.

LYING GLUTEUS STRETCH

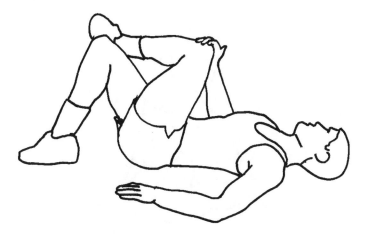

How to do it: Lie on your back with your knees bent. Place the left ankle on the right knee. Keep the right foot on the floor. Gently pull the right knee toward the left shoulder. Repeat on the other side.

Form points:
- Keep the shoulders on the floor.
- Keep the neck relaxed.

LOW BACK STRETCH

How to do it: Lie on your back. Bend both knees and lift your feet off the ground. Place your hands behind your knees and hug them into your chest while pressing your low back into the floor.

Form point:
- Keep the neck relaxed.

SEATED GLUTEUS AND HIP STRETCH

How to do it: Sit with your left leg extended at a 45 degree angle from your body. Bend the knee of the right leg and place the right foot outside the left thigh. Place your right hand behind you and the left hand on the right knee. Bend the left knee. Gently pull the bent knee toward your shoulder. Repeat on the opposite side.

Form point: • Make sure your weight is evenly distributed on each hip bone. Don't lean.

GROIN STRETCH

How to do it: Sit with your knees bent and the bottoms of your feet together. Create a space between your rib cage and your pelvis by lifting your chest and pulling in your low abdominals. Try to push your knees to the floor. Leading with your chest, lean forward at the waist.

Form points: • Relax your neck.

• Keep your chest elevated—don't lose your four-finger space.

144

PECTORALS AND ANTERIOR DELTOID STRETCH

How to do it: Stand with your fingers interlocked behind you. Pull your shoulder blades together and down.

Form points:
- Don't turtle.
- Don't pull excessively on the wrists. The objective is to pull the shoulder blades together.

SUPERMAN STRETCH

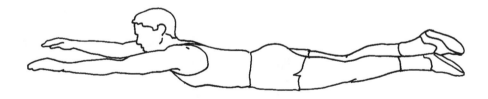

How to do it: Lie on the floor face down with your legs and arms outstretched. Lift your chest, arms, and legs simultaneously and hold.

Form points:
- Keep the neck relaxed.
- This is an advanced stretch that helps strengthen the low back. It might not be appropriate for beginners or those with very weak low backs. Try modifying it by having the client keep the legs on the floor and just lifting the chest and arms. Progress to arms plus one leg, then opposite arm and leg, and finally the version shown.

QUADRATUS LUMBORUM SIDE STRETCH

How to do it: Sit with your right leg extended at a 45 degree angle to your body and the left knee bent. The right toe should point toward the ceiling. Create the four-finger space between your pelvis and rib cage by lifting the chest and pulling in the lower abdominals. Slide the right hand next to the right calf. Straighten the left arm and reach to the ceiling. (The left arm should be next to your head.) Keeping your chest forward and your scapula in line with the spinal column, lean sideways toward the right leg. Try to get the right elbow down to the floor. Repeat on the other side.

Form points:
- Make sure the shoulder blade of the outstretched arm stays in line with the spinal column.
- Make sure the torso stays in the frontal plane.

GASTROCNEMIUS STRETCH

How to do it: Stand about 12 inches away from a wall. Place the left foot forward and extend the right foot back. Place your forearms against the wall. Lean into the wall and keep the right leg straight with the heel down to stretch its gastrocnemius. Repeat on the other side.

Form points:
- It's important to keep the heel down. If you can't, move the left leg closer to the wall. As the stretch gets easier, you can move the right leg farther away from the wall.
- Keep the pelvis straight and facing forward.
- Make sure the left knee does not extend past the foot.

SOLEUS STRETCH

How to do it: Same as gastrocnemius stretch, except that you bend the knee of the extended leg.

Form points: • Same as gastrocnemius stretch.

DOOR STRETCH

How to do it: Stand in a doorway. Flex your elbows 90 degrees and place your forearms against the door frame. With your feet behind the doorway, lean into the door space.

Form points: • Make sure that forearms stay against the door frame.

                             • Don't turtle.

POSTERIOR DELTOID STRETCH

How to do it: Place one hand just above the elbow of one arm. Gently pull the upper arm toward your chest. Switch sides.

Form points:
- Keep your scapula pulled down and in line with each other.
- Don't turtle.

INTERNAL/EXTERNAL ROTATOR STRETCH

How to do it: Standing or seated, straighten your right arm up next to your head. The upper portion of the arm should be next to your head and the forearm should be behind your back, with the palm of the hand and fingers resting on your back between the shoulder blades. Reaching down with the right arm and up with the left, try to touch a finger from each hand together between your shoulder blades.

Form point:
- If it's impossible for you to get your fingers together, use a towel and try to get a little closer together each time by inching your fingers up and down the towel.

TRICEPS AND LATERAL FLEXION STRETCH

How to do it: Stand. Lift both arms up next to your head. Flex your elbows and place each hand on the opposite arm. Exert gentle pressure on the left elbow while leaning slightly to the right. Switch sides.

Form points:
- This exercise can also be done seated.
- Do not hyperextend your neck. Keep your chin down so that your neck is in line with the spine.

Sample Forms

Waiver Form

Letter of Agreement

Health History Questionnaire

Medical Clearance and Physician's Consent to Participate in Fitness Assessment and Exercise Program

Goal Inventory

Lifestyle Questionnaire

Notes on Using the Workout Record Form

Workout Record Form

Physical Activity Readiness Questionnaire (PAR-Q)

Waiver Form

This form is an important legal document. It explains the risks you are assuming by beginning an exercise program. It is critical that you read and understand it completely. After you have done so, please print your name legibly and sign in the spaces provided at the bottom.

Waiver and Covenant Not to Sue

I,_____, have volunteered to participate in a program of physical exercise under the direction of **(Your business's name),** which will include, but may not be limited to, weight and/or resistance training. In consideration of **(Your business's name)** agreement to instruct, assist, and train me, I do here and forever release and discharge and hereby hold harmless **(Your business's name),** and their respective agents, heirs, assigns, contractors, and employees from any and all claims, demands, damages, rights of action or causes of action, present or future, arising out of or connected with my participation in this or any exercise program including any injuries resulting therefrom.

Assumption of Risk

I,_____, recognize that exercise might be difficult and strenuous and that there could be dangers inherent in exercise for some individuals. I acknowledge that the possibility of certain unusual physical changes during exercise does exist. These changes include abnormal blood pressure, fainting, disorders in heartbeat, heart attack, and in rare instances, death.

I understand that as a result of my participation in an exercise program, I could suffer an injury or physical disorder that could result in my becoming partially or totally disabled and incapable of performing any gainful employment or having a normal social life.

I recognize that an examination by a physician should be obtained by all participants prior to involvement in any exercise program. If I,_____, have chosen not to obtain a physician's permission prior to beginning this exercise program with **(Your business's name),** I hereby agree that I am doing so at my own risk.

In any event, I acknowledge and agree that I assume the risks associated with any and all activities and/or exercises in which I participate.

I acknowledge and agree that no warranties or representations have been made to me regarding the results I will achieve from this program. I understand that results are individual and may vary.

_____   _____
Participant's signature   Date

_____
Please print name

Letter of Agreement

This Agreement made and entered into this _____ day of _____, 199__, by and between _____("Client") and _____ ("Trainer").

In consideration of the mutual promises exchanged herein and other good and valuable consideration, the parties agree as follows:

(1) Client and Trainer have agreed that Trainer will conduct ___ one-hour workout sessions. Each session will begin at a mutually convenient, agreed-upon time and shall be subject to the policies attached hereto as "Exhibit A."

(2) Client will pay Trainer, in advance, the sum of $_____ for these workout sessions. Client acknowledges and agrees that no credit or refund shall be due for sessions cancelled by Client, except as provided in the Policies attached hereto as Exhibit A.

(3) Concurrently with the execution of this Agreement, Client has executed and delivered to Trainer a Waiver and Assumption of Risk Agreement, a Waiver for Home Workouts Agreement (if applicable), and a Waiver and Informed Consent for Exercise Testing (these agreements herein collectively referred to as the "Waiver Agreements"), in which Client assumes the risk of participating in an exercise program and agrees that Trainer and his or her agents, employees, or contractors, if any, shall have no liability for any injury, illness, or similar difficulty that Client may suffer arising out of or connected with Client's participation in Trainer's program. **Client hereby acknowledges and agrees that the execution and delivery of the Waiver Agreements are material inducements to Trainer's permitting Client to participate in Trainer's program.**

(4) Client and Trainer may agree to conduct additional sessions at such times and locations as they may agree upon, and in such event (i) the provisions of this Agreement, including the Policies attached hereto as Exhibit A, shall be deemed to apply to such additional sessions and (ii) Client will pay Trainer, in advance, the sum of $_____. Client acknowledges and agrees that no credit or refund shall be due for sessions cancelled by Client, except as provided in the Policies attached hereto as Exhibit A.

IN WITNESS WHEREOF, Client and Trainer have caused this Agreement to be executed on the day and year first above written.

by: _____   by:_____
                 Trainer   Client's signature

_____   _____
     Trainer, please print name   Client, please print name

POLICIES

1. Sessions last about one hour. Please be *ready to begin* at your scheduled time.

2. Time slots are available on a "first come, first served" basis by appointment. Clients who train on a monthly basis will usually have priority since they can schedule regular standing times (for example, Monday, Wednesday, Friday at 5:30 pm).

3. About cancellations

   1. During the period of your first _____ sessions ("Initial Training Period"), you will receive no credit for cancelled or missed workouts, *regardless of the reason*, unless we cancel, in which case you'll receive a free workout for every session cancelled.

   2. If you continue as a New Silhouette client after your Initial Training Period, you will pay the monthly rate and receive credit as follows:

      $_____ per session, subject to paragraphs 3-7 below

   3. You will not receive credit for any workout unless it was cancelled with at least 24 hours' advance notification. Cancellations must be given by calling 708-352-8544 to be deemed effective.

   4. You will not receive credit for more than one (1) cancelled workout per month unless we cancel, in which case you will receive credit for each cancelled workout.

   5. If you receive credit for missed workouts, you must use these credits within 60 days or they will be waived.

   6. If you are entitled to credit in accordance with this paragraph, such credit will appear on the following month's invoice and shall not be deducted from the current month's invoice.

   7. No credit shall be due if a session is cancelled due to any of the following: floods, fires, earthquakes, tornadoes, power failure, or similar severe weather conditions or acts of God making travel extremely difficult or impossible; automobile accidents involving you or resulting in your inability to arrive at your scheduled workout; or any event of similar magnitude, beyond the control of the parties. (You will still get credit if we cancel because we are involved in an accident, illness, or other difficulty.) See the following paragraph for holiday credits.

   _____
   Client's initials

4. Payment is due in advance of the first session. If you are training on a monthly basis, you will receive a statement on or about the first of the month, which is due and payable on or before the fifth of the month. If you want to train on a monthly basis but your start date is on a date other than the first of the month, you will be billed a prorated amount for the month that you start. Then you will receive an invoice on the first of the next month. If a regularly scheduled session occurs on one of the following holidays, no credit is due: President's Day, Memorial Day, the Fourth of July, Labor Day, Thanksgiving Day, Christmas Day, New Year's Day. Sometimes holidays necessitate schedule modifications. For example, the gym may close early on Christmas Eve or New Year's Eve. If you are unavailable to modify your schedule to fit in a workout under these circumstances, no credit will be due.

5. You will be required to sign and return the following forms to me before taking a fitness evaluation or beginning any program:

    a. Waiver and Assumption of Risk Form
    b. Waiver for Exercise Testing
    c. Waiver and Assumption of Risk (for Home Workouts), if applicable
    d. Health History Questionnaire
    e. Supplemental Health History
    f. Client Goal Sheet

If you have any of the following physical conditions, you will be required to have a Medical Clearance and Physician's Consent Form:

    *Hypertension (>145/95 mmHg)
    *Hyperlipidemia (cholesterol > 220 mg/dl or a total cholesterol-to-HDL ratio of > 5.0)
    *Diabetes
    *Family history of heart disease prior to age 60
    *Smoking
    *Abnormal resting EKG
    *Any other condition that I in my sole discretion may deem to present an unreasonable risk to your health, were you to participate in a fitness evaluation or program.

6. Clients will be required to keep a food diary for two weeks at the beginning of the program. After two weeks, the diary will be analyzed for nutritional content, and I will make suggestions to help you improve your diet.

7. Clients are required to observe any and all rules of the gym or facility where workouts take place.

8. Shirts and shoes are required at all times during sessions. I suggest that you also bring a towel and a lock, since these are not supplied at the gym.

9. Clients have the right to terminate a particular exercise or workout at any time. **You are in control of your workouts!** If an exercise is uncomfortable or painful, or if you want to stop for any reason, you may do so. If a particular exercise is painful for you to do or you have an injury or other limitation that makes it difficult for you to do, I can probably substitute another exercise to work that particular muscle group.

10. Clients are encouraged to drink plenty of water during the workout. You do not need my permission to get a drink or go to the bathroom.

11. You will get from your workouts what you put in. I will show you how to work your muscles correctly and encourage you to go to your safe limit, but whether you reach your goal is ultimately up to you. You are the only one who can make sure you work out consistently (missing workouts is a guarantee to get nowhere!), eat properly, rest enough, and live a healthful lifestyle.

_____

Client's signature

Health History Questionnaire

Name _____ Date _____

Street Address _____ City _____

Phone (home) _____ (work) _____

Person to contact in case of emergency: Date of birth _____

Name _____ Phone _____

For most people, physical activity should not pose any problem or hazard. The following questions are designed to identify the small number of adults for whom physical activity might be inappropriate or those who should have medical advice concerning the type of activity most suitable for them.

Common sense is your best guide in answering these questions. Please read them carefully and check the "Yes" or "No" opposite the question if it applies to you.

Yes   No

____   ____   1. Has your doctor ever said you have heart trouble? If yes, please describe the problem and state when it was diagnosed.

                    _____

                    _____

____   ____   2. Do you frequently have pains in your heart and chest?

____   ____   3. Do you often feel faint or have spells of severe dizziness?

____   ____   4. Has a doctor ever told you that your blood pressure was too high?

____   ____   5. Has your doctor ever told you that you have a bone or joint problem, such as arthritis, that has been aggravated by exercise or might be made worse by exercise?

____   ____   6. Is there a good physical reason not mentioned here why you should not follow an activity program even if you wanted to do so?

____   ____   7. Are you over age 65 and/or not accustomed to vigorous exercise?

____   ____   8. Are you or have you ever been a diabetic?

____   ____   9. Are you now or have you been pregnant within the last three months?

____   ____   10. Have you had any surgery in the last three months?

____   ____   11. Have you been hospitalized in the last two years? If so, when and why?

                    _____

____   ____   12. Have you ever seen a chiropractor, acupuncturist, or other alternative medicine practitioner? If so, when and why?

                    _____

Please check the box if you have ever experienced any of the following symptoms:

	When first experienced	Treatment used

❏ Pain or discomfort in the chest

❏ Unaccustomed shortness of breath

❏ Dizziness

❏ Labored or uncomfortable breathing, with or without pain

❏ Swollen ankles

❏ Heart palpitations

❏ Heart murmur

❏ Limping

❏ yes ❏ no Do you have high blood pressure? If yes, what is your current blood pressure without medication?

_____

❏ yes ❏ no Are you taking any medication for hypertension? If so, what medication?

_____

❏ yes ❏ no Is your total serum cholesterol level over 240?

❏ yes ❏ no Do you smoke?

❏ yes ❏ no Have you ever smoked? If so, when did you quit?

❏ yes ❏ no Do you have diabetes?

❏ yes ❏ no Do you have a family member who has had coronary or artherosclerotic disease prior to age 55?

❏ yes ❏ no Do you have pain or discomfort in your back?

❏ yes ❏ no Do you have pain or discomfort in your knee? If so, ❏ right or ❏ left?

❏ yes ❏ no Do you have pain or discomfort in your shoulder? If so, ❏ right or ❏ left?

❏ yes ❏ no Do you have pain or discomfort in your elbow? If so, ❏ right or ❏ left?

❏ yes ❏ no Do you have pain or discomfort in your wrist? If so, ❏ right or ❏ left?

❏ yes ❏ no Do you have pain or discomfort in your ankle? If so, ❏ right or ❏ left?

If you checked "yes" above, please describe your pain. On a scale of 1 to 10, with 1 being almost nonexistent and 10 being excruciating, how severe is it? Does it get more or less severe as the day goes on? When do you notice it? What really aggravates it?

_____

_____

_____

_____

❏ yes ❏ no Have you ever torn ligaments or cartilage in your knee? If so, when? _____

Did you have surgery on this knee? If so, when? _____

❏ yes ❏ no Have you ever dislocated your shoulder? If so, when?

_____

❏ yes ❏ no Have you ever had shoulder surgery? If so, which shoulder? When?

_____

❏ yes ❏ no Have you ever had a neck injury, such as whiplash? If so, when?

_____

❏ yes ❏ no Have you ever been treated for a spinal disc injury? If so, when?

_____

❏ yes ❏ no Do you ever experience tingling or numbness in your elbows or hands?

_____

What is the present state of your general health? _____

What regular physical activities do you do now? _____

How often? _____ For how long each session? _____

I, _____, certify that I understand the foregoing questions and my answers are true and complete. I also understand that this information is being provided as part of my initial consultation and may not be periodically updated.

I, _____, assume the risk for any changes in my medical condition that might affect my ability to exercise.

_____   _____
Signature   Date

If you answered "yes" to one or more questions and you have not recently done so, consult with your doctor before beginning an exercise program. Tell your doctor which questions you answered "yes" to and explain that you plan to undergo an exercise program that may include, but not be limited to, weight and/or resistance training. After medical evaluation, ask your doctor

1. which activities you may safely participate in and

2. what specific restrictions, if any, should apply to your condition and which activities and/or exercises you should avoid.

I, _____, acknowledge that I have read the foregoing statements and understand the content thereof.

_____   _____
Signature   Date

Medical Clearance and Physician's Consent to Participate in Fitness Assessment and Exercise Program

To: (Your name, address, city, state, and zip)

Dear Personal Trainer:

My patient, _____, has advised me that he or she intends to participate in (1) a fitness assessment, including body composition assessment, muscular endurance and flexibility tests, a blood pressure reading, and cardiovascular fitness assessment and (2) an exercise program, which will include, but not be limited to, resistance training. The sessions will last approximately one hour, and will begin at a very moderate, submaximal level.

Please be advised that my patient, _____, should be subject to the following restrictions in the fitness assessment and/or in his or her exercise program:

_____

_____

_____

In addition, under no circumstances should he or she do the following:

_____

_____

I have discussed the foregoing restrictions and limitations with my patient, _____, and, with these specific restrictions, he or she has my permission to participate in a fitness assessment and pursue an exercise program under your guidance.

Very truly yours,

_____   Date: _____
(Please sign name here)

_____, M.D.   Phone number _____
(Please print name here)

Client _____
Date _____

Goal Inventory

1. What I want to accomplish

These are my outcome goals for the next eight weeks:

2. Why I want to accomplish these goals

These goals are very important to me because

3. I'll do almost anything except this:

I am willing to do anything within reason to reach these goals, other than (please be as specific as possible)

4. "I think that my exercising at least four days a week, every week, is highly likely." With respect to yourself, do you

      (Please circle the appropriate #)

    1   Strongly agree

    2   Agree

    3   Disagree

    4   Strongly disagree

If you circled 3 or 4, why? (Please be as specific as possible.)

5. When I reach this goal, here's what I will get and how I will feel:

Lifestyle Questionnaire

Your Attitude Toward Food

Diets

Have you ever been on a diet? If so, please answer the following questions:

How many diets have you been on in the last two years?

_____

_____

Describe any diets you've been on. Did you go to a commercial weight loss service (Jenny Craig, Diet Center, etc.)? Did you follow a diet from a book or article? If so, which one?

_____

_____

Describe your experience with diets. Did you lose weight? Did you gain any of it back?

_____

_____

Food

❑ yes ❑ no   Do you eat breakfast?

❑ yes ❑ no   Typically, do you eat after 8 p.m.? If so, what do you usually eat?

_____

How many times a day do you eat?

_____

❑ yes ❑ no   Can you recall ever eating to avoid doing something? If so, when was this?

_____

❑ yes ❑ no   Do you ever eat when you aren't hungry? If so, when?

_____

How often do you read food labels?

_____

❑ yes ❑ no   Do you ever "treat" yourself with food? If so, when?

_____

What sources of information about nutrition have you found most helpful?

_____

❑ yes ❑ no   Has someone ever encouraged you to eat something that is not in your best interest? If yes, did you do it? Why?

_____

Your Attitude Toward Exercise: What's the Point of All of This Anyway?

    You need to create a clear, tangible image in your mind of the benefits of staying on your fitness program. It must be vivid and powerful enough to sustain you through difficult times when you feel your self-discipline and motivation slipping. This exercise will help you create that image.

Complete this sentence: "If I do three cardiovascular exercise sessions and two to three resistance training sessions per week, it will . . ."

	Not likely				Very likely	
Improve my appearance 1	2	3	4	5	6
Allow me to cope with stress better 1	2	3	4	5	6
Help me avoid getting sick 1	2	3	4	5	6
Give me a powerful sense of personal achievement 1	2	3	4	5	6
Increase my self-esteem 1	2	3	4	5	6
Improve my physical strength 1	2	3	4	5	6
Make me more independent 1	2	3	4	5	6
Improve my ability to concentrate 1	2	3	4	5	6
Take up too much time 1	2	3	4	5	6
Cause pain, soreness, and discomfort 1	2	3	4	5	6
Make me very tired 1	2	3	4	5	6
Cause me to get injured 1	2	3	4	5	6

Please rewrite this sentence and complete it in your own words.
If I do three cardiovascular sessions and two to three resistance training sessions per week, it will . . .

_____

_____

Do you need support from others (friends, family, etc.) to stay consistent with your exercise and nutrition program? ❑ yes ❑ no Do you have this type of support? ❑ yes ❑ no
On a scale of 1 to 10 (10 is the ultimate nurturing, supportive group), how much? _____

Are there people in your life who either intentionally or unintentionally discourage or interfere with your staying consistent in your exercise and/or nutrition program? ❑ yes ❑ no If yes, how do they interfere? How do you deal with it?

_____

_____

Has someone else ever interfered with your choice to exercise? ❑ yes ❑ no If yes, what happened?

_____

If you answered "yes" to questions 3 or 4, how have you dealt with these situations in the past? What are your thoughts about how to improve these responses in the future?

_____

_____

_____

"I think it is very likely that I will exercise five times a week."

	Not likely			Very likely	
1	2	3	4	5	6

"I think exercise is a waste of time for me."

	Always			Never	
1	2	3	4	5	6

"I know that I will be consistent with my fitness and nutrition program for six months."

	A certainty			Impossible	
1	2	3	4	5	6

"When I exercise, I look like a dork."

	Always			Never	
1	2	3	4	5	6

"When I exercise, I always feel beat up afterwards."

	Always			Never	
1	2	3	4	5	6

Notes on Using the Workout Record Form

1. Record the day and date of the session. While it might not seem important, sometimes you will see a pattern that will be helpful in your planning. For example, you might start to notice that a client's energy level on Mondays is distinctly lower than it is during your Wednesday workouts. Then you learn that her work schedule dictates that she be in at 6 a.m. on Mondays for a weekly staff meeting. You can use this information to adjust the intensity of Monday and Wednesday workouts.

2. Write down the time.

3. Record notes on the general warm-up.

4. Refocus your attention on what you and your client are working on during the current phase. A phase can last anywhere from three weeks to four months, depending on the client's fitness level, goals and objectives, and similar considerations.

5. Record any special needs or concerns affecting this client, such as back problems, shoulder problems, and so forth.

6. Record the order in which the exercises are performed. The reason for this should be obvious. If, for example, you are not able to do the exercises in the order you planned, your client's strength could be affected. Say you planned deadlift then leg curl, but because someone was using the power rack, you reversed the order. This change might affect the difficulty of the leg curl. Then again, it might not, but it's good to know.

7. Record the seat position or other adjustable components of any machine you use.

8. Write down the Subjective Intensity Rating for each exercise.

9. Review the workout after it's completed. Consider the client's SIR and your impression of the quality of his form and decide whether to increase the number of repetitions (+#), decrease the rest interval (-↓), increase the amount of weight (+↑), or leave things status quo (↔).

10. Make notes about anything significant that happens during the workout.

11. Abdominals have their own section because you will probably work on them every workout.

12. Record the muscle or muscle groups stretched by checking the appropriate box, and, where necessary, writing in the name of the stretch.

13. Record any aches, pains, or problems your client reports. Be as specific as possible.

14. Note any matters you want to talk to your client about.

15. Record your client's most recent weight.

16. Record your client's energy level. How do you know? You ask her at the beginning of the workout.

Workout Record Form

Client's name: _____

1. Day and date	3. Warm-up	4. Goals this phase	Grade of this workout
2. Time		5. Client's limitations, if any	

6. Order Exercise			W	1st Goal	Actual	2nd Goal	Actual	3rd Goal	Actual	9.	10. Notes
7. Machine position		Wt								+#❑ −↓❑ +↑❑	
		Reps									
		Rest								↔❑	8. SIR
Machine position		Wt								+#❑ −↓❑ +↑❑	
		Reps									
		Rest								↔❑	SIR
Machine position		Wt								+#❑ −↓❑ +↑❑	
		Reps									
		Rest								↔❑	SIR
Machine position		Wt								+#❑ −↓❑ +↑❑	
		Reps									
		Rest								↔❑	SIR
Machine position		Wt								+#❑ −↓❑ +↑❑	
		Reps									
		Rest								↔❑	SIR
Machine position		Wt								+#❑ −↓❑ +↑❑	
		Reps									
		Rest								↔❑	SIR
Machine position		Wt								+#❑ −↓❑ +↑❑	
		Reps									
		Rest								↔❑	SIR
Machine position		Wt								+#❑ −↓❑ +↑❑	
		Reps									
		Rest								↔❑	SIR
Machine position		Wt								+#❑ −↓❑ +↑❑	
		Reps									
		Rest								↔❑	SIR
Machine position		Wt								+#❑ −↓❑ +↑❑	
		Reps									
		Rest								↔❑	SIR

11. Abdominals

Exercise					
Reps	Rest	Reps	Rest	Reps	Rest
Reps	Rest	Reps	Rest	Reps	Rest

12. Flexibility		13. Aches, pains, problems:	15. Weight _____ on _____ (date)
❑ Hamstrings	❑ Pectorals		
❑ Upper back	❑ Low back		
❑ Neck	❑ Calf	14. Discuss with client:	16. Energy level:
❑ Hips	❑ Triceps		
❑ Groin	❑ Shoulder		
❑ Biceps	❑ Hip abduction/adduction		
❑ Internal/external shoulder rotators			

Physical Activity Readiness Questionnaire (PAR-Q)

1. Has your doctor ever said you have a heart condition and recommended only medically supervised physical activity?

2. Do you have chest pains brought on by physical activity?

3. Have you developed chest pain within the last month?

4. Do you tend to lose consciousness or fall over as a result of dizziness?

5. Do you have a bone or joint problem that could be aggravated by the proposed physical activity?

6. Has a doctor ever recommended medication for your blood pressure or for a heart condition?

7. Are you aware, through your own experience or a doctor's advice, of any other physical reason against your exercising without medical supervision?

Fitness Testing

Body Composition

Percent Fat Estimates for Three Sites—Men
Age to last year

Sum of three skinfolds	18-22	23-27	28-32	33-37	38-42	43-47	48-52	53-57	>58
8-12	1.8	2.6	3.4	4.2	4.9	5.7	6.5	7.3	8.1
13-17	3.6	4.4	5.2	6.0	6.8	7.6	8.4	9.1	9.9
18-22	5.4	6.2	7.0	7.8	8.6	9.3	10.1	10.9	11.7
23-27	7.1	7.9	8.7	9.5	10.3	11.1	11.9	12.6	13.4
28-32	8.8	9.6	10.4	11.2	12.0	12.8	13.5	14.3	15.1
33-37	10.4	11.2	12.0	12.8	13.6	14.4	15.2	15.9	16.7
38-42	12.0	12.8	13.6	14.4	15.2	15.9	16.7	17.5	18.3
43-47	13.5	14.3	15.1	15.9	16.7	17.5	18.3	19.0	19.8
48-52	15.0	15.8	16.6	17.4	18.1	18.9	19.7	20.5	21.3
53-57	16.4	17.2	18.0	18.8	19.6	20.3	21.1	21.9	22.7
58-62	17.8	18.5	19.3	20.1	20.9	21.7	22.5	23.3	24.1
63-67	19.1	19.9	20.6	21.4	22.2	23.0	23.8	24.6	25.4
68-72	20.3	21.1	21.9	22.7	23.5	24.3	25.1	25.8	26.6
73-77	21.5	22.3	23.1	23.9	24.7	25.5	26.3	27.0	27.8
78-82	22.7	23.5	24.3	25.0	25.8	26.6	27.4	28.2	29.0
83-87	23.8	24.6	25.3	26.1	26.9	27.7	28.5	29.3	30.1
88-92	24.8	25.6	26.4	27.2	28.0	28.8	29.6	30.3	31.1
93-97	25.8	26.6	27.4	28.2	29.0	29.8	30.5	31.3	32.1
98-102	26.7	27.5	28.3	29.1	29.9	30.7	31.5	32.3	33.1
103-107	27.6	28.4	29.2	30.0	30.8	31.6	32.4	33.2	33.9
108-112	28.5	29.3	30.1	30.8	31.6	32.4	33.2	34.0	34.8
113-117	29.3	30.0	30.8	31.6	32.4	33.2	34.0	34.8	35.6
118-122	30.0	30.8	31.6	32.4	33.1	33.9	34.7	35.5	36.3
123-127	30.7	31.5	32.2	33.0	33.8	34.6	35.4	36.2	37.0
128-132	31.3	32.1	32.9	33.7	34.4	35.2	36.0	36.8	37.6
133-137	31.9	32.7	33.4	34.2	35.0	35.8	36.6	37.4	38.2
138-142	32.4	33.2	34.0	34.8	35.5	36.3	37.1	37.9	38.7
143-147	32.9	33.6	34.4	35.2	36.0	36.8	37.6	38.4	39.2
148-152	33.3	34.1	34.8	35.6	36.4	37.2	38.0	38.8	39.6
153-157	33.6	34.4	35.2	36.0	36.8	37.6	38.4	39.2	39.9
158-162	33.9	34.7	35.5	36.3	37.1	37.9	38.7	39.5	40.3
163-167	34.2	35.0	35.8	36.6	37.4	38.1	38.9	39.7	40.5
168-172	34.4	35.2	36.0	36.8	37.6	38.4	39.1	39.9	40.7
173-177	34.6	35.3	36.1	36.9	37.7	38.5	39.3	40.1	40.9
178-182	34.7	35.4	36.2	37.0	37.8	38.6	39.4	40.2	41.0

Percent Fat Estimates for Three Sites—Women
Age to last year

Sum of three skinfolds	18-22	23-27	28-32	33-37	38-42	43-47	48-52	53-57	>58
8-12	8.8	9.0	9.2	9.4	9.5	9.7	9.9	10.1	10.3
13-17	10.8	10.9	11.1	11.3	11.5	11.7	11.8	12.0	12.2
18-22	12.6	12.8	13.0	13.2	13.4	13.5	13.7	13.9	14.1
23-27	14.5	14.6	14.8	15.0	15.2	15.4	15.6	15.7	15.9
28-32	16.2	16.4	16.6	16.9	17.0	17.1	17.3	17.5	17.7
33-37	17.9	18.1	18.3	18.5	18.7	18.9	19.0	19.2	19.4
38-42	19.6	19.8	20.0	20.2	20.3	20.5	20.7	20.9	21.1
43-47	21.2	21.4	21.6	21.8	21.9	22.1	22.3	22.5	22.7
48-52	22.8	22.9	23.1	23.3	23.5	23.7	23.8	24.0	24.2
53-57	24.2	24.4	24.6	24.8	25.0	25.2	25.3	25.5	25.7
58-62	25.7	25.9	26.0	26.2	26.4	26.6	26.8	27.0	27.1
63-67	27.1	27.2	27.4	27.6	27.8	28.0	28.2	28.3	28.5
68-72	28.4	28.6	28.7	28.9	29.1	29.3	29.5	29.7	29.8
73-77	29.6	29.8	30.0	30.2	30.4	30.6	30.7	30.9	31.1
78-82	30.9	31.0	31.2	31.4	31.6	31.8	31.9	32.1	32.3
83-87	32.0	32.2	32.4	32.6	32.7	32.9	33.1	33.3	33.5
88-92	33.1	33.3	33.5	33.7	33.8	34.0	34.2	34.4	34.6
93-97	34.1	34.3	34.5	34.7	34.9	35.1	35.2	35.4	35.6
98-102	35.1	35.3	35.5	35.7	35.9	36.0	36.2	36.4	36.6
103-107	36.1	36.2	36.4	36.6	36.9	37.0	37.2	37.3	37.5
108-112	36.9	37.1	37.3	37.5	37.7	37.9	38.0	38.2	38.4
113-117	37.8	37.9	38.1	38.3	39.2	39.4	39.6	39.8	39.5
118-122	38.5	38.7	38.9	39.1	39.4	39.6	39.8	40.0	40.0
123-127	39.2	39.4	39.6	39.8	40.0	40.1	40.3	40.5	40.7
128-132	39.9	40.1	40.2	40.4	40.6	40.8	41.0	41.2	41.3
133-137	40.5	40.7	40.8	41.0	41.2	41.4	41.6	41.7	41.9
138-142	41.0	41.2	41.4	41.6	41.7	41.9	42.1	42.3	42.5
143-147	41.5	41.7	41.9	42.0	42.2	42.4	42.6	42.8	43.0
148-152	41.9	42.1	42.3	42.8	42.6	42.8	43.0	43.2	43.4
153-157	42.3	42.5	42.6	52.8	43.0	43.2	43.4	43.6	43.7
158-162	42.6	42.8	42.0	43.1	43.3	43.5	43.7	43.9	44.1
163-167	42.9	43.0	43.2	43.4	43.6	43.8	44.0	44.1	44.3
168-172	43.1	43.2	43.4	43.6	43.8	44.0	44.2	44.3	44.5
173-177	43.2	43.4	43.6	43.8	43.9	44.1	44.3	44.5	44.7
178-182	43.3	43.5	43.7	43.8	44.0	44.2	44.4	44.6	44.8

Sit-and-Reach Test for Hamstring Flexibility

The most widely used test for low back and hamstring flexibility is the sit-and-reach. It certainly has its deficiencies, the principal one being that it fails to take into account individual differences in torso and arm length. Someone with very long arms or a long torso will get a higher score because of these structural characteristics that have nothing to do with flexibility in the hamstrings and low back. That having been said, these deficiencies are problematic only when you view the test as a means for comparison of one person to another. Where you are comparing Client A on day 1 versus day 60, these deficiencies disappear. The test is 100 percent valid for comparing changes in an individual client's flexibility.

You can do this test either with a commercial flexibility box or with a yardstick and tape measure. If you choose the latter, which is more portable, tape the yardstick to the ground (tape perpendicular to the yardstick) at the 15-inch mark. Have your client sit with the yardstick between his legs and your heels at the 15-inch mark. His feet should be 10 to 12 inches apart. Have him bend at the waist, drop his head forward, and reach with one hand on top of the other as far as he can. It's important that he keep his knees straight and not rotate at the torso, which is the reason you ask him to place one hand on top of the other. Do the test three times and take the best result.

Rating	Females			Males		
Age	46+	36-45	35 and less	46+	36-45	35 and less
Excellent	22	23	23	20	22	21
Good	19	21	21	17	19	19
Above average	18	19	20	15	16	17
Average	15	17	18	13	14	15
Below average	14	14	15	11	12	12
Fair	11	12	14	8	10	9
Poor	9	10	11	5	5	7

Adapted by permission of the YMCA of the USA from *The Y's Way to Physical Fitness* by Lawrence Golding, Clayton Myers, and Wayne Sinning, Copyright © 1989 (Champaign: Human Kinetics Publishing). Copies of the book may be purchased from the YMCA Store at 1-800-747-0089.

Finger-Touch Test for Rotator Cuff Flexibility

The subject should be wearing a tank top or be shirtless. After the general warm-up and a brief specific warm-up (arm circles), have her stand with her back to you. Have her reach up toward the ceiling with her left arm next to her head, then, keeping the left upper arm stationary, flex the left elbow and place her left hand against her upper back. Place the right hand behind the back and reach up with the back of the hand against the back. The objective is to touch the fingers behind the back. Measure and record the distance between the fingers. Perform the test of the opposite side by reversing the hand and arm positions.

Scoring
(Distance between fingers in inches)

	Males	Females
Excellent	0-1	0-.5
Good	1-3	.5-2.5
Average	3-4	2.5-4
Poor	4-10	4-10

Author's Note: This table is derived from my measurements of a variety of individuals of all ages. It's less important where your client falls on the scale than whether he or she is improving from test to test.

Three-Minute Step Test

Equipment needed: 12-inch box or bench, metronome, stopwatch

This test was developed by the YMCA. While it does not test $\dot{V}O_2$max, it does give a rough estimate of cardiovascular fitness by measuring the heart's rate of recovery.

How to do it: Set the metronome to 96 beats (24 steps) per minute and the stopwatch to three minutes.

Demonstrate this technique to your client: Keeping pace with the metronome, step up with your right foot, up with your left, down with your right, and down with your left. Allow your client to practice by stepping in time. You can keep track of the client's heart rate one of two ways—either locate your client's radial pulse (I suggest you mark it with a felt-tip pen) and take it manually, or have your client wear a heart monitor during the test. Advise your client that he should feel free to stop stepping any time he feels dizziness, lightheadedness, chest pain, nausea, or for any other reason. Have your client begin stepping and start the timer. After time expires, have your client sit down and take his pulse for one minute. His score is his resting pulse after one minute.

Many unconditioned middle-aged people can't complete the full three minutes, either because of orthopedic problems (knee or back pain) or because their heart rates climb like a NASA booster rocket and they are too exhausted to continue. You will notice that the client is no longer able to keep up with the metronome and can no longer speak. In this case, you should stop the test, then record the ending pulse rate and the amount of time completed. On the retest, your goal will be to complete the full three minutes, or at least a greater percentage than he completed the last time.

Norms for Three-Minute Step Test
(One Minute Recovery Heart Rate)

	Women			Men		
	18-35	**36-55**	**56-85**	**18-35**	**36-55**	**56-85**
Excellent	72-90	74-95	74-92	70-82	72-88	72-88
Good	91-102	86-105	83-103	83-88	89-98	89-96
Above average	103-111	106-116	104-116	81-100	89-108	97-103
Average	112-120	117-120	117-122	101-108	108-117	104-113
Below average	121-128	121-126	128-128	109-118	118-123	114-121
Fair	129-135	127-137	129-134	118-129	124-134	122-132
Poor	136-154	136-152	135-151	130-164	135-158	133-152

Adapted by permission of the YMCA of the USA from *The Y's Way to Physical Fitness* (3rd ed.) by Lawrence Golding, Clayton Myers, and Wayne Sinning, Copyright © 1989 (Champaign: Human Kinetics Publishing).

Push-Up Test for Upper-Body Strength

This test measures upper-body (pectorals, deltoids, and triceps) strength and endurance. Men do the traditional push-ups with the toes tucked under and the hands shoulder-width apart and straight under the shoulders when the arms are straight. Women are permitted to do the test on their knees (upper-body position is the same.) Have your client get into the straight-arm position. Place your fist on the floor just below the client's sternum. The client must, while keeping the back perfectly straight, lower his or her chest down to touch your fist. The test is terminated when the client can no longer do these push-ups with perfect form. The score is the total number of push-ups completed.

		Score at age				
		20-29	30-39	40-49	50-59	60+
Men						
	High	>45	>35	>30	>25	>20
	Average	35-44	25-34	20-29	15-24	10-19
	Below average	20-34	15-24	12-19	8-14	5-9
	Low	<19	<14	<11	<7	<4
Women						
	High	>34	>25	>20	>15	>5
	Average	17-33	12-24	8-19	6-14	3-4
	Below average	6-16	4-11	3-7	1-5	1-2
	Low	<5	<3	<2	0	0

Reprinted with the permission of Simon & Schuster, Inc. from *Health and Fitness Through Physical Activity* by M.L. Pollock, J.H. Wilmore, and S.M. Fox. Copyright © 1978 (New York: McMillan Publishing Company).

Curl-Up Test for Abdominal Strength

Most of us remember that sit-up test from when we were kids. We paired up with a partner who held our feet while we attempted to do as many sit-ups as possible within a given number of minutes. As many of you know, the problem with this test is that the hip flexors, not abdominals, do most of the work when the feet are anchored. The curl-up test was developed in an attempt to make the test more specific to abdominals.

The client lies on his back, arms by the sides, palms down on the floor, elbows rigid, fingers straight, knees flexed at 90 degrees. Measure three inches away from the longest fingertip of each hand and mark this spot with tape. The client performs the test by curling his head and shoulders up while keeping the feet and fingers on the floor for one minute.

Keep in mind that this test is less a matter of quantitative precision than it is a rule of thumb to see if your client is getting stronger. More curl-ups in one minute with good form demonstrates that your program is strengthening his power core.

Scoring

Excellent	>48
Good	36-48
Average	24-35
Below average	16-23
Poor	<16

SUGGESTED READING

As terrific as this book is, I didn't have time or space to include all of the books that you should read to be a professional personal trainer. Fortunately, both you and I can benefit from the knowledge, wisdom, and experience of the following authors. I encourage you to read these books. Not only will your knowledge increase dramatically, but you will be reminded of the complexity and miraculousness of the human body and the importance of your calling.

Alter, Michael. 1988. *Science of stretching*. Champaign, IL: Human Kinetics.

Alter, Michael. 1990. *Sport stretch*. Champaign, IL: Human Kinetics.

Very useful books with illustrations of stretches for every part of the body.

American College of Sports Medicine. 1995. *Guidelines for exercise testing and prescription*. 5th ed. Baltimore, MD: Williams & Wilkins.

A manual for professionals from the premier certifying organization, this guide contains information about testing and programming for the general population and those with special needs.

Anderson, Bob. 1987. *Stretching*. New York: Random House.

One of the first popular books about stretching, updated since its first (1980) publication. It contains some basic physiology about stretching, as well as some specifics on stretching for a variety of conditions.

Anderson, Kristen, and Ron Zemke. 1991. *Delivering knock your socks off service*. New York: American Management Association.

Personal training is a service business, and this little book will give you invaluable tips about being a customer service star.

Baechle, Thomas R., and Barney R. Groves. 1992. *Weight training: Steps to success*. Champaign, IL: Human Kinetics.

A wonderful book that takes you through each step of designing an effective and safe weight training program. Contains formulas and charts to help you select appropriate weights, reps, sets, and rest periods.

Bailey, Covert. 1978. *Fit or fat*. Boston: Houghton Mifflin.

Bailey was one of the first experts to recognize, explain, and popularize what is now considered common knowledge: There is a difference between overweight and overfat. He explains why an event, such as eating a candy bar, is neutral: Its effect depends on whether one is "fit or fat." An excellent book for reviewing the physiological relationship between diet and exercise. Great to recommend to clients, too.

Also recommended: *The Fit or Fat Woman*, Houghton Mifflin Company, 1986 and *Fit or Fat Target Recipes*, Houghton Mifflin Co., 1989, both by Covert and Lea Bailey.

Cooper, Kenneth, M.D. 1991. *The aerobics program for total well-being*. New York: Bantam Doubleday.

As the cover proclaims, Dr. Cooper is "the man who started America running." In this book, he identifies three components of total well-being: exercise, diet, and emotional balance. He explains his point system for comparing various aerobic activities, which is quite useful for clients who cross-train. Contains many useful references.

Corbin, Charles B., and Ruth Lindsey. 1993. *Concepts of physical fitness*. 8th ed. Dubuque, IA: Brown & Benchmark.

This book stresses health-related fitness. It explains each concept with factual information, graphs, tables, and a glossary of terms for each chapter. In addition, it contains over 25 labs for studying everything from physical activity to being an informed fitness consumer.

Donatelli, Robert A., ed. 1991. *Physical therapy of the shoulder*. 2nd ed. New York: Churchill Livingstone.

A book intended for physical therapists. It discusses flexibility, posture, and common injuries to the most mobile joint in the body.

Fleck, Steven J., and William J. Kraemer. 1987. *Designing resistance training programs*. Champaign, IL: Human Kinetics.

A very serious book from two of the leading authorities on resistance training. It contains a lot of heavy, scientifically based information that you can use in program design. An essential addition to your professional library.

Gavin, James. 1992. *The exercise habit*. Champaign, IL: Human Kinetics.

This book approaches exercise motivation by analyzing the fitness incentives that push different individuals' buttons. Is it concern for appearance? Sociability? What is the role of self-esteem? The book contains questionnaires for figuring out what motivates your client.

Gavin, James, and Nettie Gavin. 1995. *Psychology for health fitness professionals*. Champaign, IL: Human Kinetics.

A little gem. A book that will help you understand your clients, support them, and effectively communicate with them.

Golding, Lawrence, Clayton Myers, and Wayne Sinning. eds. 1989. *The Y's way to physical fitness: The complete guide to fitness testing and instruction*. 3rd ed. Champaign, IL: Human Kinetics.

This book is invaluable when doing your fitness testing. It contains all the information you need to use calipers correctly, to do a bench-step cardiovascular test, as well as other specific testing protocols. Another must-have!

McArdle, William, Frank I. Katch, and Victor Katch. 1991. *Exercise physiology, energy, nutrition, and human performance*. 3rd ed. Philadelphia: Lea & Febiger.

This was a textbook used during my master's program, but not a week goes by that I don't consult it still. It explains the complex information about energy use and exercise capacity in a clear, understandable way. It provides scientific theory and fact, but also suggests practical uses for this information.

National Strength and Conditioning Association. 1994. *Essentials of strength training and conditioning*, Champaign, IL: Human Kinetics.

Thomas Baechle, executive director of the Certified Strength and Conditioning Specialist Agency, the certifying body for the National Strength and Conditioning Association (NSCA), edited this book. He is also a veteran competitive weightlifter and powerlifter. In short, this guy knows his stuff. He and a group of highly qualified contributors have created an extremely valuable resource for the fitness professional who wants to help clients achieve optimal performance safely and effectively. Highlights include a great section on program design.

Nieman, David C. 1990. *Fitness and sports medicine*. Palo Alto, CA: Bull.

This text contains everything you need to know about exercise physiology and testing. It has oodles of useful tables, illustrations, questionnaires, and forms. Each chapter has a comprehensive list of references that can point you in the right direction if you want to do research on a particular topic.

Pearl, Bill, and Gary Moran, PhD 1986. *Getting stronger*. Bonia, CA: Shelter Publications, Inc.

A comprehensive illustrated manual of weight training. Contains useful sections on popular sports and suggests exercises to improve performance in each.

Rasch, Phillip J. 1993. *Kinesiology and applied anatomy*. 7th ed. Baltimore: Lea & Febiger.

This textbook provides a good overview of kinesiology, the study of movement, and reviews basic biomechanical and physical laws that help you understand the effects of resistance training. It contains a whole section on the various body systems generally affected by resistance training.

Rejeski, Jack W., and Elizabeth A. Kenney. 1988. *Fitness motivation: Preventing participant dropout*. Champaign, IL: Human Kinetics.

This book summarizes current information from the fields of psychology and sociology about motivation and compliance. It will help you answer the questions "Why don't they do what they know they're supposed to?" and "How can I help them do better?"

Sewell, Carl, and Paul B. Brown. 1992. *Customers for life*. New York: Pocket Books.

The message seems obvious: Give the customer what she wants. Obvious or not, you will learn a lot about serving your clients from this book.

Westcott, Wayne. 1993. *Be strong*. Dubuque, IA: Brown & Benchmark.

Wayne Westcott is one of the leading experts in the field of strength and resistance training. This well-written book contains illustrations of all the joint movements, and some very useful information about understanding your client's potential strength by understanding the effect of muscle length and tendon insertion points.

Westcott, Wayne. 1994. *Strength fitness: Physiological principles and training techniques*. Dubuque, IA: Brown & Benchmark.

This book is more technical than *Be Strong*. It appears to be written for a professional or academic audience. One of the best parts is the chapter on research in the area of strength training.

Wilmore, Jack, and David Costill. 1994. *Physiology of sport and exercise*. Champaign, IL: Human Kinetics.

A comprehensive college text on exercise physiology. An essential for your professional library.

Teri O'Brien is the founder and president of New Silhouette, a fitness consultation firm located in the Chigago area. Since starting the company in 1991—shortly after completing her master's degree in exercise science at the University of Illinois at Chicago—she has designed optimum performance programs for people of all ages and conditions. A variety of women's and professional groups have enjoyed her entertaining talks and workshops on effective exercise programming, personal effectiveness, successful aging, and optimum performance.

Teri is not your usual fitness expert. Coaching and motivational speaking is a second career for this self-described recovering lawyer, who practiced law for seven years. In 1976 she received her bachelor of arts degree at Arizona State University (ASU), where she graduated summa cum laude and Phi Beta Kappa. She discovered the energy-boosting and stress-busting powers of exercise while she was in law school at ASU. To relieve her anxiety from school pressures, Teri began running and continued for nearly 10 years, completing five marathons and dozens of 10K races. After abandoning running in favor of weight training, Teri competed in several bodybuilding competitions, including the Gateway Classic, where she placed fourth in the lightweight class.

Teri is certified as a health fitness instructor by both the American College of Sports Medicine and the American Council on Exercise. In addition, she is a member of the National Strength and Conditioning Association.